Staff of Life

Real Artisan Bread at Home

by

Simon Thomas

This book is
dedicated to my
long-suffering,
talented and
beautiful wife,
Julie, without
whom there would
be no Staff of Life
Bakery.

By way of introduction...

There are a number of things which you may feel are obvious when making bread and indeed even in speaking about bread.
Be assured that this book is not a grandmothers' egg-sucking manual and be patient or skip ahead as you see fit, according to your existing knowledge and ability in the craft.

I promise there will be no chapter devoted to the battery of gadgets which purport to transform your homemade loaves into world-class artisan breads with little or no effort or inspiration.

If such baubles were really as effective as the marketing claims there would be no need for a book like this or indeed a baker like me.

The chapter with small piles of flours, grains, nuts, fruits, seeds and all manner of ingredients is likewise conspicuous by its absence. I will cover the main grains used in making bread and some more interesting ones which you may enjoy playing with but the ingredients of bread are simple and may be augmented or limited by your own imagination and requirements as you become more familiar with the techniques and styles available to you.

When you grasp the nature of breadmaking and can feel the qualities of the dough in your hands, you will find your ingredients suggest themselves to your subconscious mind even during the mixing itself.

You will find new possibilities for flavours and textures which you just know will work beautifully with your intended meal.

Draw inspiration from diverse sources and never be afraid to experiment to test your instincts. The price of ingredients is generally fairly low and your results will rarely, if ever, be inedible. The knowledge gained from such 'play' is of inestimable value and the mistakes will soon be outnumbered by the instinctive, innovative creations which will make your heart sing.

Your friends and family will be both your best critics and your most appreciative, and often voracious, focus group. Learn from their reactions to your efforts but rather than turn your hand to producing the comfortable fluffy white pap that many people think they prefer, try to combine flavours and complement your breads with preferred foods like good quality bacon and sausages.

Who can resist a steaming bacon or sausage sandwich or a delicious rarebit made more glorious by the use of real bread, fresh from the oven and with the scent of baking mingling with the cooking smells from the stove?

I have lost count of the number of customers who have begged a piece of dough to bake in their home oven when trying to sell a house, to lend it that comfortable air of 'home' rather than mere 'house'. The taste and the smell of fresh bread enchants us all on a level so instinctive that we immediately become involuntarily hungry.

The baker who is truly gifted is a genuine and rare blessing deserving respect as a true craftsperson and an asset to the whole community.

I began making bread during stays with my Grandma in Yorkshire when I was very young. She was a baker of white tin loaves only, that being the variety which my Grandad preferred. The dough was of course made by hand in the ubiquitous Mason Cash baking bowl which seemed to have a place in so many kitchens where baking was an almost daily occurrence.

Once shaped, the loaves were put into well-greased (with a butter wrapper) tins, blackened by many years of use, and placed in front of the fire covered with a tea towel to rise until baking in an ancient gas oven.

Grandma's bread was always fresh and delicious and also inspired my mother to bake her own bread at home. I have always been spoiled by eating good bread so when I went to university in 1980 I had little option but to make my own. Once I had got used to baking the usual brown and white tins, I started to experiment with ingredients and was soon hooked.

I spent quite a few years in sales jobs of various descriptions before taking the plunge and opening a small café-restaurant with my wife Julie. What made the café special was the fact that breads would be hand-made fresh every morning ready for service later in the day. I was able to experiment with my recipes each day and soon built up both a repertoire of bread styles and flavours and an appreciative and discerning core of customers ready to buy my bread.

Encouraged by the expectant queue of Real Bread purists at our door each morning, we decided to devote all our energies to baking bread for retail sale on a market stall in Kendal. We closed the café. Trade was brisk and we were baking as much as we could from home, so when our local pizzaolo suggested that we might like to use his big oven in the mornings we leapt at the chance.

We soon reached capacity there too, so with the help of Made in Cumbria we opened the Staff of Life Bakery in the tiny Berry's Yard in the middle of town. We are still there today and many of our original customers from the café are still buying our bread. We think that fact speaks volumes for our products and our relationship with our customers. It's one of the things that makes us love the business we have built over the last 18 years.

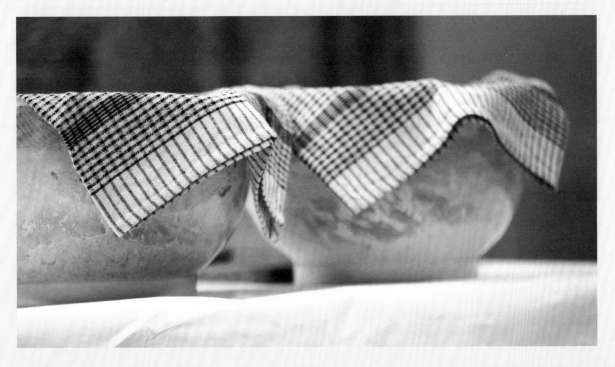

Contents

What you really need

Ingredients.

At its most basic all you really need is flour and water but given that we want to make the first loaf an easy one, and one which will appeal to your family and friends, you will need a little more.

Flour.

Best to start with wheat flour.

Water.

Unless the tap water in your neighbourhood is foul tasting it will be just fine. If it really is undrinkable use still bottled water. Fizzy water will not make your bread rise any quicker.

Yeast.

You can use fresh yeast, often available in delis and at supermarket deli counters these days, or dried active yeast in sachets or in bulk.

Salt.

Regular table salt or cooking salt is fine. Expensive varieties of sea salt are equally effective.

That will do just fine. For now.

Equipment.

An oven; electric, gas, solid fuel, take your pick... anything but microwaves is good. A kettle, or other means of heating water other than the hot tap. A bowl, or a trough to mix in, and also to rest the dough in and contain it while it proves. The old-school artisans used wooden troughs. Plastic is perfect; ideally your bowl should be semi-transparent so you can see the bubbles as the dough proves. Pyrex or Mason Cash stoneware are suitable too.

A jug to mix and pour the water. At least one hand. A flexible plastic semi-circular bowl scraper. A baking sheet or bread tin; ideally one which has been much used (new tins tend to stick easily). Brush with oil or butter wrapper. A sieve is handy for dusting surfaces ready for kneading. A wooden or plastic hoop with fine nylon mesh construction is best. Oven gloves, or an oven cloth. We use welders' gloves at the bakery.

Attitude.

Be in a good mood, with an open and receptive mind. The mood will be enhanced as you continue with the breadmaking, trust me.

Basic technique

This is the stuff you really need to know to use this book effectively. Please give it a try exactly as described here when you make the first few loaves. After that please feel free to tweak my techniques to suit your own style of working and adapt the recipes likewise.

But for starters, follow this tried and tested method and handmade bread will be achievable and accessible to most people. And it's how we do it at Staff of Life Bakery.

The doughs will seem to be very wet and sticky at first, compared to the average home-made mix. The extra hydration is one of the things which sets professional artisan-baked loaves apart from the domestic variety. More water equals more steam in the oven and a looser structure in the loaf will give you a far more interesting crumb and texture as well as a more appealing crust.

Persevere with the techniques and your breads will turn heads and raise smiles at your table. Timing is the other factor which may seem very different from the usual regime. The virtues of extended bulk proving have been shown to deliver more flavour and nutritional value as well as a better structure and the flexibility to use less salt or yeast in the original mix.

The other bonus is that you can do the initial 10 minute mix, cover the bowl then go out to work and deal with the rest on your return. On the other hand the excuse that you don't

make your own bread because you don't have the time will no longer be available to you.

Step One. It is a good idea to follow the classical French system of *'mise en place'*, which means that the things you will need for the mix should be assembled at the very beginning. An incidental benefit of this method is that it removes the possibility that you do not have, or have run out of, an essential ingredient.

After all, in a family home there's always the risk of someone finishing the milk in the fridge or scrambling the eggs you were saving for that special enriched loaf.

It is a good idea to either wear an apron or old casual clothes. Have your ingredients ready weighed out into bowls if you prefer. You should have a bowl to mix in and some warm water ready in a jug. If you are right-handed put the jug on your left. Do the initial mixing with just one hand, keeping the other clean and dry so that you can pour dry ingredients, operate scales, turn the bowl round and dispense pocket money while you work.

Put all the dry ingredients into the bowl, mix thoroughly and make a deep well in the centre. If you are using fresh yeast rather than dry, just crumble it into the bowl once the salt has been well mixed in. Direct contact with salt will kill fresh yeast. The dried variety is more robust.

The water in your jug should be warm rather than hot. How warm is debatable and slightly irrelevant as the yeast will multiply anyway. Slightly cooler water will mean that the rise is slower but as we are using a bulk proving time of several hours anyway it is unlikely to be noticeable.

Pour the water into the well a little at a time and start to combine the ingredients using a circular movement of your hand whilst turning the bowl with your free hand. It is very important at this stage that you do not try to bring the dough together into a ball. For now we're not kneading, just combining the ingredients into a well-hydrated dough.

Your mixing hand should be a paddle, helping the flour to absorb more water by turning the mix around and over until it is all wet. Be sure there is not a pile of dry flour in the bottom of the bowl by turning the dough over a couple of times during mixing.

When you have added almost all the water called for, feel the dough. It should be soft and fairly sticky and definitely NOT pulling away from the sides of the bowl. If it has formed a tight smooth ball it is not sufficiently hydrated. Wheat flour takes time to absorb the liquid and your mixing will be accomplished in only a few minutes, so be aware that the dough will dry out slightly as it absorbs liquid.

This effect is much more pronounced when using wholemeal wheat and rye flours, whole cracked grains and dried fruits. It is a shame to ruin a lovely bread by having it crack alarmingly in the oven due to a lack of moisture at the first stage.

Do not be frightened of wet doughs. They allow you scope to play with the texture of breads and develop more flavour. Once your dough is properly hydrated, cover it with a dry clean tea towel or clingfilm and leave it

for at least five hours to develop gluten, taste and texture. In the bakery, most of our bread is left for 12-15 hours to bulk prove, which means we can cut the yeast to around 2.5 teaspoons for a 30kg mix and bring salt down to less than one per cent. This improves the flavour and makes our style very distinctively handmade as well as being considered healthier.

When it has proved for the first time, you will notice lots of bubbles in the dough. Ideally at this stage they should be small and plentiful. The dough may also seem very sticky indeed. This is not a problem and is easily handled.

Next, put some flour in your sieve and dust the work surface well. An even layer is the more important than quantity, so practice will make perfect. Use your plastic scraper to loosen the dough from the sides of the bowl and then invert it so that the dough reaches out to the floured surface. Finish loosening the dough with the scraper, leaving an unruly mass of dough ready for kneading.

This is the really important bit!

Kneading the dough is the heart of breadmaking and without mastering it you will never be able to produce the loaves you dream about.

The technique we use at Staff of Life is based upon only three simple movements and acts in harmony with the dough rather than fighting it and creating tension in the bread. Once the dough is lying in a formless heap on

the floured surface the first stage is to gather it into a more regular shape by folding the sides in towards the centre. This also serves to coat the whole thing in flour.

If the dough is very wet and sticky you may need to use a scraper, otherwise try and keep your hands flat like paddles and well-floured so you can move the dough without getting hold of it. If you try to grip a wet dough the outer skin will break and you will become stuck to it very quickly, whereas a 'bat' with a paddle-hand will soon bring it into a floured ball shape.

If you want a good demonstration, just watch a cat playing with a ball and emulate its movements when getting to grips with the dough.Once your dough is in the form of a flattish round or oval you can start the kneading proper. Keep some flour to hand and dust the surface as required; little and often is the way.

First steps

First Movement

Using both hands together, flip the opposite edge of the dough towards you so that it folds in the centre like a billfold style wallet.
DO NOT PRESS IT DOWN OR TIDY IT UP AT ALL.

Second Movement

Roll the whole piece of dough away from you using both hands but applying very little downward force. As the dough becomes firmer and more resilient during kneading it will need a little more pressure. To increase the pressure use the weight of your shoulders rather than the strength of your arms. It should roll without tearing so it is vital that your hands move together in harmony with the motion of the dough. **DO NOT ATTEMPT TO MAKE IT LOOK TIDY OR SHAPE IT AT ALL.**

Third Movement

Give the dough a quarter turn in the horizontal plane only. It is vital that you do not turn the dough over at any stage of the kneading process. It is also important that the whole piece of dough turns through 90 degrees and is not stuck to the work surface. If it sticks, loosen it with your scraper and add a little flour underneath.

Return to First Movement

Continue the series of three movements until you feel the texture of the dough begin to change under your hands. Because of the repetitive nature of the kneading technique you will find that you can detect minute changes in the feel of the dough very quickly and you will soon know instinctively when the kneading is complete.

Using this style it is difficult to over-knead because of the gentle and sympathetic nature of the movements. It is, however, rather hypnotic and can lead to a seriously addictive contemplative state. Set your kitchen timer for ten minutes or so to make sure you don't nod off!

Ten minutes kneading is over the top. Three or four minutes will be plenty in most cases. There are many descriptions of the texture of well-kneaded dough but the one which works for me is this. The dough when first gathered together is like a flabby tummy, loose and almost fluid.

When properly ready it feels more like a well-toned muscle, resilient and firm. The other method I like is the ear test. Well-prepared dough, when pinched gently between forefinger and thumb, should feel like your earlobe. It's weird but seems to work.

Shaping the dough is easy, particularly if you are aiming for a boule or a bloomer style. When you judge the dough to be ready, just flip the whole lump over. You will find that it has stretched itself into an almost perfect circle.

To create the boule shape imagine that the dough is a football. Cup your hands, palms upwards, at the base of the ball and start to turn it at the same time as undercutting it with your hands. It will form a sphere very quickly.

Transfer this to a baking sheet and leave in a warm place to rise. To make a bloomer shape, start as above and, on reaching the boule stage, simply rock the dough from side to side very gently, allowing it to become an oval by itself. The more you rock, the longer the oval. Then transfer to a tray for the final rise in a warm place.

If you prefer to use a tin or bread pan, the shaping is also very simple. Knead as above into a spherical shape. Then rock to start it turning oval. When the dough is the length of the bottom of your chosen tin just tuck your fingers under the ends of the oval to turn them under slightly before placing the dough gently in the tin.

There is no need to force the dough down into the tin because, providing you're using a properly hydrated mix, it will find its own way into the corners and up the sides with no assistance.

Put the baking sheet or tin somewhere warm to rise. An airing cupboard or a heated greenhouse are ideal. However the shelf over the Aga, a warm room or a propagator with a lightbulb for heat source are fine too. Keep it from draughts and try to use a place where the warmth comes from below or from all directions, avoiding the windowsill where all the heat comes from one side only.

My Grandma baked fantastic bread risen in front of a coal fire, which should be one of the worst places for the purpose. Some bakers can make anything work; Grandma Thomas was one of them.

To bake your loaf, ensure that the oven is at the correct temperature then glaze the top or sprinkle with additions as you see fit. Slash it

with a sharp knife and slide gently into the oven, closing the door carefully behind it without slamming.

Such care is necessary to avoid the little jolts which cause the very fragile layer of bubbles at the bottom of your loaf to collapse under its weight, leaving a dark unsightly line across the bottom of every slice. It's not terminally damaging and has no effect on the flavour but it will annoy you to bits, I promise.

Most loaves of 400g to 800g will take 30-45 minutes to bake through at the correct oven temperature. Lighter white loaves will bake quickest and heavy multigrains and rye breads slowest.

Take note of the recommended oven time then set your timer for five minutes less. Your domestic oven could be 10 per cent hotter or cooler than the temperature stated on the gauge.

Other factors like the hydration of the dough can also affect the speed of baking. No two bakers will make exactly the same loaf from the same set of instructions and ingredients. Only machines can do that.

To test whether your loaf is done all the way through, take it from the oven, turn it over and tap the bottom of the loaf. Some people knock with their fingers, some tap like a bongo drum. I use the side of my thumb in the manner of some bass guitarists.

What we are all listening for is the same - a slightly hollow sound as if playing a wooden drum. In time you will also feel the resonance in a loaf to confirm the sound test is accurate.

I have won money from professional bakers using this technique as opposed to following a rigid prescription on time and temperature. It is the only way to be sure that you are not going to make a fool of yourself by serving a loaf of bread at your table only to find it's half-baked. And yes, that is where the expression comes from.

If, after testing, you judge that the loaf is not yet ready, put it back in the oven for another five minutes then repeat the whole process. If still not done, repeat until you have added 20 minutes to the recipe timing. At this stage the loaf should certainly be

cooked unless your oven is not functioning properly. Take it out anyway. Remove the loaf from the baking sheet or tin. If it is stuck, use a palette knife to loosen it and remember to grease the tin/sheet better next time. Put the loaf on a wire rack to cool slowly.

Try and resist the temptation to cut it while still hot from the oven as this will not only leave you with an ugly doughy slice of bread, it will spoil the look of the whole loaf. There is an exception to this, and it comes in the shape of the pull-apart style of breads such as fougasse and focaccia, which are better eaten warm. If you have the self-restraint to hold back, many loaves will develop more flavour and a better texture after a few hours. I rarely eat my bread on the day it is baked. I prefer it the next day when the flavours are set and the texture is firmer. It slices thinner too.

If you want your bread to have a soft crust, brush it with melted butter or oil when it comes out of the oven, and cover it with a clean tea towel. Crusty breads are not everyone's cup of tea.

If on the other hand you live only for the crisp thick crust, pop your loaf back into the oven with the door open until they are both cool. This will dry the crust out and make it bark as you slice it.

Incidentally, most big bakery plant tins have lids to keep the steam in which means there is no crust at all, just a sickly brown skin to contain what they optimistically describe as a loaf.

Many craft bakers are seeking enhanced volume by the use of overproving in a steam cabinet before baking, resulting in a loaf with little structure and a tendency to collapse and tear when butter is applied. The tin loaf is extremely useful for toast, for sandwiches and for freezer space. It is overlooked and underrated. Your first foray into the real artisan bread style will produce a familiar style of bread.

The difference will be in the crust, the texture of the crumb, the scent of wheat and yeast combined, and in the love baked into every slice. If you need further convincing, grill some back bacon and make bacon sandwiches fit for heroes.

My Grandma baked fantastic bread risen in front of a coal fire, which should be one of the worst places for the purpose. Some bakers can make anything work; Grandma Thomas was one of them.

The list of ingredients for this next recipe is short

The method is as in the previous chapter so I will keep that part of it very brief too. It's as near as we will get to a quick loaf!

It is an honest loaf with no pretensions. Everyone will bake it and eat it over and over again.

This is the first bread that I made with Grandma Thomas and the first one that my son Joe made with me at the bakery. I pass it on to you and yours.

You're never too young to have a go. I learned to bake as a small child, standing on a painted wooden stool in my Grandma's tiny kitchen in Redcar. I could just reach the worktop to knead teacakes for Grandad's "bait bag" so that he could have fresh bread for his lunch.

My own son learned to make bread when he was so small that we had to stand him on a stool at the bakery so he could knead the dough.

Grandma Dawson cut down one of the Staff of Life Bakery aprons and a hat to fit him so he looked the part. He loved working alongside me and sometimes finds time in his busy life to help me still. But he somehow always finds time to eat my bread.

You will need a pair of 1lb bread tins as the quantity given will make two good small tin loaves. If you can come by some old tins that have already got a reliable patina on them the resulting crust will be better. You will also need a pair of scissors.

Ingredients

600g good quality strong white wheatflour
(see the section at the back for trusted sources)

8g salt

1 teaspoon active dried yeast

30g softened butter
(vegan alternative 3 teaspoon vegetable oil)

440ml warm water

Extra flour for dusting and kneading

Method

First prepare tins by brushing with oil or use a butter wrapper. Measure the dry ingredients into a bowl and make a well in the centre. Put the softened butter/oil in the bottom of the well. Pour in water to fill the well and begin to loosely combine the ingredients.

As the water is taken up by the flour add more with your free hand. Mix until you have a sticky loose dough. Cover the bowl and prove in a suitable place for 2-3 hours. Inspect the dough for bubbles. If they are plentiful, turn out the dough onto a floured surface for kneading. If there are only a few bubbles, leave the dough to rise for another 30 minutes.

Knead the dough until it starts to become more resilient. Divide in two and knead each half until it feels elastic and toned. Shape into two ovals, tuck the ends under and put into the tins. Put the tins in a suitable place for the final proof.

Heat the oven to 220°C. When the dough has risen to 0.5 cm below the rim of the tin it is ready to go in the oven. Using a pair of scissors, gently cut down the centre line of the loaf to a depth of 2mm.

Put in the middle of the oven, reduce the temperature to 190°C and bake for 30 minutes. Test the loaf after 25 minutes by tapping the bottom and listening for the resonance. If it requires longer, return to the oven for five minutes. If still not done put it back once more.

After 40 minutes, the loaf will be done, so remove it from the tin and set to cool on a wire rack. Dust the top with flour if you like a farmhouse style or rub over with a butter wrapper for a softer crust. Wait 20 minutes before summoning the devourers of bread to admire your skill and creativity. Get a good sharp bread knife and make sure that you save the first slice for yourself. If you don't, you may never get to taste it at all.

You may feel it prudent to hide the second loaf but they will probably find it anyway. It is for eating and not for the freezer after all. Who needs to freeze it now you can make it so easily?

And then...

How to make it more interesting for your audience

Audiences like tricks and showboating and things like miniature loaves. Nothing wrong with that at all but it helps if you can surprise them once in a while too.

Try playing with dried fruits as an inclusion in your plain white doughs but resist the obvious and be unpredictable in your choice. Dried apple, for instance, when chopped coarsely, tossed in cinnamon and included in a well-hydrated overnight dough, will assume the consistency of lightly cooked fresh apple. A delightful alternative to using fresh apple, which will produce a rather nasty uncooked texture in the dough immediately around it.

Plain chocolate too can be added to the dough in chunks for a luxurious loaf. Use the good stuff, with a cocoa content over 60 per cent so that the taste pervades the whole loaf. Make sure that the chocolate chunks stay on the inside of the loaf, as any which are left out in the heat of the oven will be lost. Milk or white chocolate tend to be just sweet and cloying and contribute nothing to the flavour of the bread. If you are using good plain chocolate, perhaps add a pinch of chilli, a sprinkle of *fleur du sel*, or some ground spices, which will help to distinguish your *pain au chocolat* from the rest.

There are many reasons to include citrus fruits in your breads. The ascorbic acid in them is a natural dough conditioner which helps dough take on a silky texture and makes it easier to handle. The flavours of orange, lemon and lime work well in bread. Use the juice, the zest and the pulp to extract the full flavour of the fruit. Add a few drops of orange flower water to intensify the scent when you bake and consider using the fruits in roughly chopped chunks too.

Fruits and nuts work well together and have a bonus of adding texture to the slice. Try orange, dates or ready-to-eat baby figs with walnuts; lemon, morello cherries or sultanas with almonds; giant flame raisins with roughly chopped Brazil nuts; and golden raisins with hazelnuts. When adding nuts to your breads you will get a better flavour if you

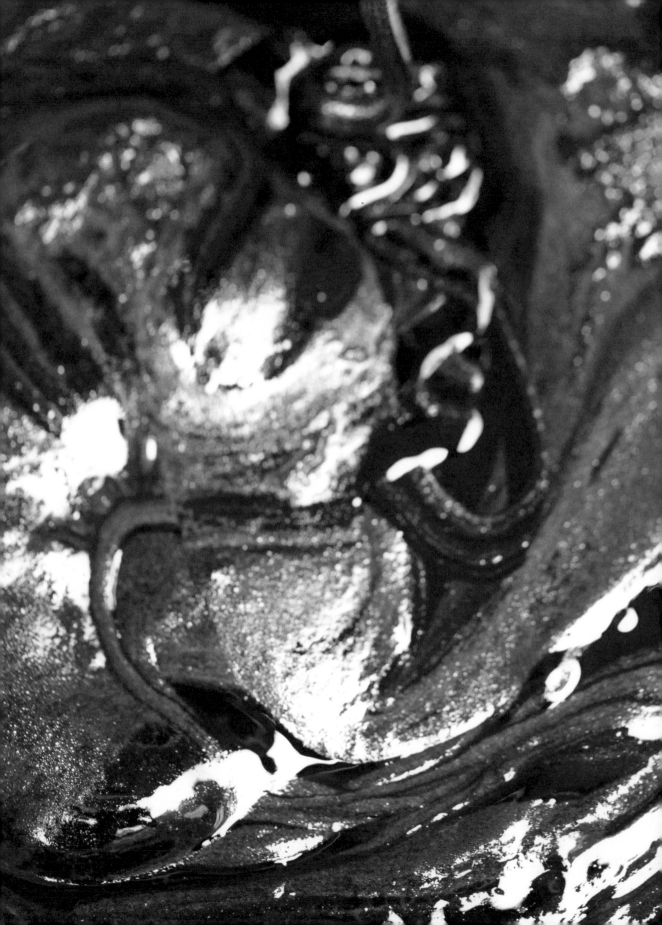

toast them briefly in the oven or a hot dry frying pan before mixing. The exception is walnuts, which benefit from a soak in walnut oil or milk before use. This allows them to absorb some of the moisture they have invariably lost during storage or transport and regain a little of their former glory.

Sweetness in your breads will almost always meet with general approbation but again try to be less predictable. When using fruit, assess the sweetness of the fruit itself before you add more sugar. A little sugar goes a long way in terms of sweetness but contributes little to the flavour or texture of the loaf. Other saccharides may add more character so why not try agave syrup, maple syrup, varietal honeys, less refined cane sugars, treacle, molasses and even golden syrup? All of these have a distinctly different effect on both flavour and crumb which may be further enhanced by using the same sugar to make a wash to glaze the crust before baking.

The addition of eggs gives breads a luxurious crumb and usually gives a boost to the oven 'spring' - the fast rise achieved when the loaf goes in the oven. Most of the world's great festival and celebration breads feature eggs in profusion. Without its eggs, the sublime Jewish Sabbath braided challah would be just another white loaf, and the classic French brioche would not work at all.

Use free-range eggs for your baking and try to build a relationship with your local supplier so that they will tip you off when the double-yolk eggs are available to add extra richness to your mixes. Eggs should be added cautiously to your breads until you are familiar with the way they work. Even a couple of eggs will make a big difference to a small mix like that in the previous section, and remember that the more eggs you add, the more cake-like your bread will become. This has the effect of making the loaf light and luxurious but will also give it a tendency to stale quickly, so have a few recipes up your sleeve to deal with any leftovers.

The other big feelgood factor to introduce to your focus group of appreciative tasters is fat. Fat, in this case, is not a feminist issue, but a classic addition to your baking arsenal and almost invariably a Good Thing. Fat conditions the dough, making it easier to handle as well as imparting a gloss to the loaf which makes it more attractive, while also improving the keeping qualities. Breads containing fat make better toast too, as they are slower to dry out under the grill, whilst browning more quickly to produce the perfect combination of crisp surface with soft moist interior which makes toast the most satisfying of comfort foods.

The traditional English bread fat is lard, which has lately fallen out of favour but was for centuries an essential ingredient in British breads and pastries. Certainly every baker worth his salt should make at least one lardy cake during his lifetime.

This classic English treat is a crossover between bread and cake with a delicious moist texture and startling longevity. It is not a health food or a weight loss snack but it is part of our national archive of recipes and deserves a place in your repertoire by virtue of taste, texture and its singular construction.

Butter will add richness and moisture to the bread but it is best to use the unsalted variety to avoid having to recalculate the amount of salt in your recipe. The amount of flavour you gain from the addition of butter is directly proportional to the quality. Bargain basement blended butter from the cash and carry will never have the sophistication of the fresh butter from your local dairy. I remember when we first started selling our bread on local 'farmers markets' there was a lovely lady who used to sell handmade butter from her own dairy herd, wrapped simply in greaseproof paper. Her unsalted butter was perfect for baking; creamy and full of richness and flavour, although its keeping qualities were minimal. Brioche made with Sue's butter was sublime; the flavours complex and sophisticated with a nutty undertone.

Eggs should be added cautiously to your breads until you are familiar with the way they work

The Happy New Year Toastie

This loaf comes into its own in the Thomas household during January. Christmas is such a high-octane culinary rollercoaster that I usually feel the need to revert to peasant food as soon after the turkey as possible. My number one choice is always toast and butter. Toast done under the grill and real butter just starting to melt on it is one of my all-time favourites, especially as a post-Christmas restorative. It is also a favourite in our house for toasted sandwiches and for filling lunch boxes with cheese sarnies.

Method

Dissolve the treacle in the warm milk. Mix all the dry ingredients together in a bowl and make a well in the centre. Add the milk and mix to a smooth dough, topping up with warm water as necessary. Cover the bowl with clingfilm and put it in a warm place to rise for two hours. Grease a 2lb loaf tin or a large baking sheet.

Turn the risen dough out onto a little flour and knead briefly. Shape it into an oval and put into the tin or divide into two ovals for the baking sheet. Cover with oiled clingfilm and prove somewhere warm for two hours or until the dough is level with the top of the tin.

Heat the oven to 200°C.

Remove clingfilm. Slash the crust once with a sharp blade as you please.

Bake in the centre of the oven for ten minutes then turn the oven down to 180°C and bake for a further 25 minutes. Test the loaf for readiness by tapping the bottom. It should resonate if it is done. If not, return it to the oven and bake for up to another ten minutes, checking after five.

Cool on a wire rack.

If you prefer a soft crust, rub the loaf with a butter wrapper while it is still warm.

Once you have tried this one you will make it again and again. It works well as a fruit loaf by adding 200g of dried fruit too. Bear in mind the affinity of caraway and rye for oranges. This loaf is divine with marmalade, but also works well as an orange loaf with the addition of a couple of liquidised Seville oranges. If you use fresh oranges, you will need to reduce the milk by 50ml.

Ingredients

400g strong white breadmaking flour

100g rye flour

5g salt

10g caraway seeds, crushed lightly

1 level teaspoon dried yeast

300ml warm whole milk

2 tablespoons treacle

Up to 100ml warm water

Hazelnut & Apricot Bread

This loaf was inspired by the delicious hazelnut and raisin flutes at Le Pain Quotidien in London's Covent Garden. It is important that you use whole hazelnuts and big chunks of unsulphured dried apricot to get the best out of this recipe. It is truly sublime with fresh soft cheeses and lovely to snack on with just some good butter.

Method

Grease two large baking sheets. Mix the dry ingredients in a bowl and make a well in the centre. Dissolve the honey in the warm milk then beat in the eggs and add to the flour, mixing gently and adding the water as required to produce a slightly sticky dough. Cover the bowl and prove for three to four hours in a warm place. Knock back, divide the dough in two and knead each until it is smooth and elastic. Shape each piece into a long oval and put them onto the baking sheets. Brush the tops with a little water and prove for one hour in a warm place. Heat the oven to 210°C. Brush the loaves with water, or with egg wash if you prefer and slash three times diagonally with a razor blade to allow the loaves to spring in the oven. Bake for 45 minutes, turning the temperature down to 190°C after ten minutes. Cool on a wire rack.

Ingredients

300g strong white bread flour

200g strong wholemeal bread flour

1 teaspoon Fermipan or 15g fresh yeast

8g salt

150g whole hazelnuts

150g dried apricots, chopped roughly

2 large free range eggs

300ml warm whole milk

2 tablespoons honey

200ml warm water

Extra flour for kneading

Classic Spelt Loaf

I'm a huge fan of spelt bread purely for reasons of flavour. I love the slightly honeyed fragrance and the caramel notes which make it such a great loaf for toasting and eating with a little good butter and some quality honey. I am fortunate to know several beekeepers who treat me to the odd honeycomb in a jar with its honey every now and then. There is just no comparison between this and the sterile anonymous honey blended to fill jars on supermarket shelves. Seek out your local apiarist and you will instantly see what I mean.

Over the years there have been numerous claims concerning the nutritional virtues of spelt. It has even been said that it is suitable for coeliacs, which is simply untrue. There is no doubt, however, that it is not the easiest flour to make bread with. It can be very slow to rise and becomes dry with very little overbaking. Once you have mastered it the flavour and texture are wonderful and it is often suitable for people with a real or perceived wheat intolerance.

Method

Dissolve the honey in 100ml of warm water. Mix the dry ingredients together in a large bowl. Make a well in the centre and pour in the honey solution and the olive oil. Add another 200ml of warm water and mix thoroughly, using more warm water as required to create a soft, slightly sticky dough. The dough should be pliable but not wet.

Cover the bowl with plastic wrap and prove at room temperature for 4-6 hours.

Turn the dough out onto a well-floured surface and knead lightly for two or three minutes.

Be careful not to crush the life out of it - spelt is not as robust as regular wheat doughs and a common complaint is that it fails to rise after kneading. Invariably this is the result of an over-enthusiastic pummeling from a baker who is more used to very strong Canadian breadmaking flours full of gluten.

Divide the dough into two pieces. This will make two 2lb tin loaves or two good round cobs.

Prepare well-greased tins or trays as you prefer and mould the loaves accordingly. Prove at room temperature for an hour.

Heat the oven to 180°C.

Gently brush the loaves with milk and sprinkle with a little flour for a rustic finish.

Bake at 180°C in the centre of the oven for 40 minutes before testing by a knock on the base of the loaf. Cool on a wire rack.

This recipe also works well with the addition of dried fruit. Raisins and sultanas work especially well, but be aware that they will absorb lots of moisture during proving, so add a little extra water in the mix or pre-soak the fruit for an hour.

Ingredients

1kg wholemeal spelt flour (we mix Watermill and Gilchesters 50/50)

12g salt (we actually use about 10g but it is quite sticky and hard to handle)

1 teaspoon dried yeast

1 tablespoon good wild honey

50ml olive oil

650ml warm water (you probably won't need it all)

Spelt Ring Loaf

You don't have to use spelt flour for this recipe. The technique works equally well with plain white dough or indeed a combination of different doughs. Use fruit and nuts or have a savoury version with olives, tomatoes, cheeses, chorizo, garlic and wild mushrooms. Let your imagination run riot. Children enjoy different coloured doughs using tomato purée, pesto, egg yolks, beetroot, etc. If you don't have a tube pan a 2lb loaf tin or 9-inch cake tin will be fine too.

Method

Dissolve the honey in the warm milk. Mix the flour, salt and yeast in a bowl, then make a well in the centre and add the oil and milk. Mix, adding water as needed, until you have a slightly sticky dough, then turn out and knead briefly until smooth and elastic. Prove in a warm place for two hours, then turn out onto a floured surface and divide into walnut-sized pieces. Knead each briefly then flatten into a disc. Add a little filling and pinch the dough together to make a round bun. Set aside for 20 minutes.

Butter the tin generously and scatter with flaked almonds. Layer the buns in the tin, brushing each with honey glaze, until 2cm below the rim. Glaze the top and sprinkle with almonds. Cover with plastic wrap and prove in a warm place for two hours. Heat the oven to 200°C while loaf rises. Turn the oven down to 180°C and bake the loaf on the middle shelf for 45 minutes. Turn out to cool on a wire rack.

Lovely toasted with jam or just sweet butter. Play around with the colours, flavours and textures of this one and you'll have lots of fun.

Ingredients

500g spelt flour

7g salt

1 teaspoon Fermipan dried yeast

1 tablespoon honey

300ml warm milk

3 tablespoons vegetable oil

Up to 100ml warm water

Filling

50g hazelnuts, toasted

25g chopped dried apricots

25g sultanas

20g flaked almonds

1 tablespoon honey dissolved in 3 tablespoons warm water to glaze

New York Deli-style Rye Bread

Method

Combine the dry ingredients in a bowl and make a well in the centre. Add all the malt and water mix. Mix the liquid into the flour, adding more as the water is absorbed. The mix should be slightly sticky but you may find that you don't use quite all the water. Leave the mix uncovered for 10-15 minutes as the cracked grains will absorb liquid more slowly than flour. Check the hydration, adding the extra water if necessary. The mix should be a little firmer than when you left it to rest. Allow the mix to prove, covered, at room temperature for three hours, or halve the quantity of yeast and allow to prove overnight for 12 hours. Heat your oven to 220°C. Turn the dough out onto a floured surface and knead until you judge it to be suitably toned. Divide the dough in two and knead each one briefly before shaping into a long oval loaf and putting on a baking sheet. Allow to rise in a warm, draught-free place for one hour. Gently brush the crust with one egg white beaten with a teaspoonful of water. (Sprinkle with caraway, sesame, or poppy seeds if you like them.) Slash the crust from end to end with a razor, lame, or very sharp knife. Transfer to the centre shelf of the oven. Turn the oven down to 200°C and bake for 40 minutes. Check by tapping on the base. If not done, return to the oven for up to another 15 minutes. Cool on a wire rack.

This bread keeps well and makes great toast too. Try it for bacon sandwiches and for toast and marmalade. Or get some pastrami, dill pickles and mustard and go to town.

This mix is also very amenable to the addition of other ingredients like fruit and nuts. It is popular in the bakery when flavoured with orange peel and sweetened with a tablespoon of honey. It makes very good rolls too if you want them for dinner.

Ingredients

450g good quality strong white breadmaking flour

150g rye flour

50g cracked wheat or cracked rye

8g salt

25g caraway seeds

1 teaspoon active dried yeast Fermipan

1 tablespoon malt extract dissolved in

300ml warm water

150ml warm water

'Light' Brioche

I love brioche as an ingredient for other dishes but it is so rich that I tend to avoid it for day-to-day consumption. This version is a little lighter and less rich than most, and is a little better for toasting due to its lower butter content. It is light enough to use for sandwiches and toast, but rich enough to impress when you incorporate it into special dishes.

For a couple of fun ways to use this bread check out the section named Perfect Partners at the back of the book.

Method

Blend the flour, salt, yeast and sugar in a bowl and make a well in the centre. Add the eggs and 200ml of the milk and mix to form a smooth, pliable dough, adding more milk as necessary. Cover the bowl and set to prove in a warm place for two hours. Turn the dough out onto a floured surface and dot it with the cubed butter, kneading lightly for a few minutes to combine all the ingredients. Return to the bowl and cover. Bulk prove at room temperature for four hours, then knead lightly on a sparsely-floured board. The dough should look glossy and feel smooth and pliable. Grease two 800g bread tins or two brioche moulds. Divide the dough in half and mould into balls for the brioche moulds or ovals for the tins. Put in the tins and brush with a little of the beaten egg yolk.

Allow to rise at room temperature for two hours or until the dough has filled the moulds.

Pre-heat the oven to 200°C. Brush the loaves with the egg yolk wash twice more and then bake at 200°C for ten minutes before lowering the temperature to 180°C for a further 35 minutes. The crust should be a dark shiny chocolate brown when the loaf is done. Turn out onto a wire rack to cool.

You can make this recipe overnight very easily by doing the bulk prove at 10°C or putting it in the fridge for 12 hours. It will slow the final prove down a little, but the flavour will be more buttery.

Ingredients

1kg strong white bread flour

12g salt

2 teaspoons dried yeast or 30g fresh yeast

1 tablespoon golden caster sugar

4 large free range eggs

500ml cold full fat milk (you may not need all of it)

250g unsalted butter, cubed and softened slightly

3 egg yolks, beaten with a teaspoon of cold water and a pinch of salt (for glazing)

The Yellow Fruit Bread

Method

Mix all the dry ingredients except the dried yeast together in a bowl. Make a well in the centre. Add the olive oil.

Dissolve the molasses and the dried yeast in the milk and add to the flour mix. Blend the ingredients together, adding water as necessary until you have a slightly sticky dough. Don't worry, the dates will absorb the extra water and leave the dough perfect. Cover the bowl and allow to rise in a warm place for two hours or at cool room temperature overnight. Turn out onto a floured board, divide the dough in two and knead into long oval loaves. Put on a greased baking tray and set aside to rise for half an hour in a warm place. Heat the oven to 220ºC. Brush the crust with milk and dust with a little flour then slash once lengthwise with a sharp blade. Put in the oven and turn the heat down to 190ºC. Bake in the middle of the oven for 45 minutes. Check the loaves are fully baked and cool on a wire rack.

This Portuguese-inspired bread is lovely with cheeses of the softer camembert style or rustic goats' cheeses. It also makes fantastic toast and keeps well at room temperature.

Ingredients

300g white breadmaking flour

200g wholemeal bread flour

100g maize meal or polenta

8g salt

4 tablespoons olive oil - a nice fruity one works best

1 tablespoon molasses (or black treacle)

300ml warm whole milk

1.5 teaspoons active dried yeast

150ml warm water

60g roughly chopped dates

40g broken walnuts

or

70g broken walnuts

30g finely chopped orange peel

Light Brown Loaf

Method

Mix the dry ingredients together in a bowl and make a well in the centre. Add the oil, honey and 400 ml of the water. Mix into a dough, adding more water as necessary, until you have a smooth texture and all the liquid is absorbed. You may not need all the water. Set aside for 10-15 minutes and check hydration, adding more water if needed. Cover the bowl and put it to prove in a warm place for three hours or halve the yeast and prove at room temperature for 12 hours. Turn out onto a floured surface and knead until firm and elastic. Divide in two and knead briefly then shape and place in oiled tins or on an oiled baking sheet and prove in a warm place for one hour. Heat the oven to 220°C. Slash the crust with a sharp blade, transfer to the oven, turn the oven down to 180°C and bake for 40 minutes. Cool on a wire rack.

This dough is great for playing around with. Add fruit, nuts, spices and grains to make it more interesting as you feel suitable.

This is the perfect sandwich bread for lunchboxes when you want a little more substance to your sarnies. It works with everything.

Ingredients

300g white breadmaking flour

300g wholemeal flour (preferably stoneground)

8g salt

1 teaspoon active dried yeast

2 tablespoons extra virgin olive oil

450ml warm water

1 tablespoon honey

Bread Bowls

These are so easy to make and look so impressive on the table that they merit a space in the freezer for emergency fine-dining opportunities or impromptu breakfasts. If, like me, you love the combination of creamy fresh scrambled eggs and succulent hot-smoked salmon, this is the perfect way to serve it - a warm crisp toasty bowl of luxury.

They are also great for a light lunch or a fun starter for your menu. Perfect for picnics too and the size is variable, so the bowls can be individual or made in a large cake tin for sharing.

Ingredients

(Makes 1-8, depending on your chosen size)

650g strong white breadmaking flour

1 teaspoon Fermipan dried yeast

Half teaspoon salt

1 teaspoon mixed dried herbs

50ml extra virgin olive oil

(plus another 50ml for brushing later)

350ml warm water

Method

Mix the dry ingredients in a bowl. Make a well in the centre and add the olive oil and 100ml water. Mix the water in gradually until you have a slightly sticky dough.Cover with plastic wrap and set aside to prove at room temperature for 4-6 hours. Choose what size you want to make your bread bowls. The ones shown here would make a substantial lunch or picnic main course. Oil four 4-inch deep cake tins or pork pie tins. (If you don't have these, small deep cake tins are fine too). Turn the dough out and knead on a floured surface for 2-3 minutes and then divide into quarters. Knead each piece into a ball. The dough should feel smooth and elastic. Put the dough in tins and set in a warm place for two hours to rise. It should be domed and near the

top of the tin. Brush with olive oil and bake for
30 minutes.

Remove from the tin and check by knocking
the base. Cool on a wire rack. When cool, cut off
the domed top and hollow out the loaf, leaving a
6-8mm thick wall and base. Brush the inside
with olive oil and bake in a hot oven for 15
minutes, then leave in to cool slowly. For a quick
lunch fill with dressed leaves, feta, olives,
anchovies, chicken, bacon, etc. Put the top back
on for a surprise dinner side-dish.

See the Perfect Partners section at the end of
the book for a great way of showing off with
these which takes only a few minutes to prepare,
This size suits a main course but they work in
muffin tins too. If the standard English summer
dampens your enthusiasm for salad-style dishes,
the bread bowls are also wonderful with thick
stews like goulash. Use your imagination.

Forager's Spring Rolls

Not a spring roll in the Chinese tradition but just as tasty. The pesto is fabulous as a stir-through pasta sauce too, so make plenty whilst the wild garlic is young and fresh.

This quick and easy recipe is fun to make with children as it involves foraging as well as baking. The rolls are easy to make and look as spectacular as they taste. They take the spiral shape of a Chelsea bun but are served up as a savoury roll for picnics or as an accompaniment for soups and salads.

Method for the pesto

Put all the ingredients into a food processor or blender and blend until smooth. You can leave it a little coarse if you prefer the texture to be more authentically Italian. If the wild garlic leaves are towards the end of the season or are quite large, it's a good idea to trim off the spine of the leaf as they can get quite tough and fibrous.

Store in an airtight jar in the fridge for up to a week.

Ingredients

For the pesto

60g toasted hazelnuts

70g wild garlic leaves, rinsed and patted dry

60g hard tasty cheese (I love to use Thornby Moor Allerdale goats' milk smoked; you may prefer Parmesan or good mature cheddar)

150ml extra virgin olive oil or (lighter) rapeseed oil

Salt and freshly-ground black pepper to taste (my advice is to go light on the salt - no surprise, I'm sure! - and heavy on the pepper)

For the rolls

Take 500g white bread dough made to your normal recipe but using only half the salt - this is important, as the pesto tastes quite salty in spite of the fact that it doesn't contain very much

Method for the rolls

Allow the dough to rise once as normal, then knock it back and knead briefly. Set aside for 20 minutes to rest.

With a rolling pin, roll out the dough into a rectangle 3mm thick, about 20 x 30 cm. Spread the dough with pesto, which should take about four tablespoons. If you have some in the pantry, a handful of toasted pine kernels adds a touch of luxury to the filling.
Roll up the dough like a Swiss roll, starting with the long side. You should be left with a cylinder about 30cm long.

Pinch the seam shut tightly with your fingers and using a sharp knife, cut it into 12 or 13 even pieces, as if you were preparing sausage rolls. Try to use a guillotine action with the knife rather than a slicing cut. It gives a cleaner finish.

Put them cut side up in a 10-inch greased sandwich tin or roasting tin. Put in a warm place to rise for two hours or until they fill the tray. Heat oven to 220°C and bake in the centre for five minutes, then turn down to 180°C. Bake for another 25 minutes until golden brown. Cool on a rack and serve warm or cold.

The remaining pesto can be used as a sauce for pasta or with grilled chicken or fish on the barbecue. It also works as a salad dressing or a salsa verde if you let it down with equal parts of lemon juice and olive oil.

The wild garlic is at its best between April and July so make the most of it! Remember to forage away from the roadside and out of the way of dog walkers for obvious reasons. If you aren't sure what wild garlic looks like there is plenty of help on the internet. If in doubt, trust your nose. If it smells like strong garlic, you have the right plant.

Stoneground Wholemeal Bread

I am often asked which bread I make for my own home at Christmas. This is one of my favourites - a lovely coarse wholemeal with some deep dark flavours and startling longevity. It goes well with all the usual Christmas starters and cheeseboards but is also a little oasis of simplicity in the luxurious expanse of festival foodie treats.

I use local flour from Carrs and the Watermill at Little Salkeld to get the best from the flavours of the wheat and to guarantee enough gluten for a good texture and spring. You can use your own local mill. It's important that the flour is coarsely ground and 100 per cent wholemeal, but also that there is enough gluten to give a good texture too. This recipe makes two small or one large tin loaf. If you double up, increase the yeast by only 50 per cent.

Method

Grease one or two bread tins with a little oil or a butter wrapper.

Measure out the molasses and dissolve in 250ml of the water.

Mix all the dry ingredients in a large bowl, make a well in the centre and put in the butter or oil. Pour in enough of the molasses water to fill the well and loosely combine the ingredients. Add more water with your free hand as required and mix until you have a sticky dough. It will feel quite coarse on your hand. Be sure to mix thoroughly so that all the flour gets wet. Wholemeal fours in general, and coarse stoneground ones in particular, absorb liquid quite slowly, so the dough will become less wet after proving.

Cover the bowl with plastic wrap and prove for four hours at room temperature or overnight in a cool place. It is a very forgiving dough, and doesn't mind a very long bulk rise as long as it is cool.

Turn out onto a floured surface and knead until the dough feels toned and resilient.

Divide the dough in two if using loaf tins. Shape into ovals and put in the tin in a warm place for an hour to rise.

Pre-heat the oven to 200ºC.

Bake in the centre of the oven at 200ºC for five minutes before turning it down to 170ºC for a further 30-35 minutes before tapping the bottom of the loaf to check it is done. If not, return it to the oven for another five minutes and check again. Don't give it more than 55 minutes. Cool on a wire rack.

Note that the crust will naturally be quite dark and is better a little overdone rather than under.

This bread freezes well for three months but keeps for a week anyway.

Enjoy it cut thickly with good butter, or cut it thin for smoked salmon and pâté. The strong wheat flavours are enhanced by the addition of molasses and make this loaf perfect for any fine cheese board.

Ingredients

300g Carrs Breadmaker Wholemeal Flour

(or another very strong wholemeal bread flour)

300g Watermill Stoneground Wholemeal Flour

(or another coarse strong stoneground

wholemeal bread flour)

8g fine sea salt

1 teaspoon active dried yeast (or 30g fresh yeast)

40g butter

2 tablespoons blackstrap molasses

400ml warm water

Exploration:

The Pursuit of Excellence

Your pursuit of excellence is not a race that you are ever going to win. It is an ongoing development of your skill, imagination and understanding. It's like the master in the martial art of judo who returns full-circle to a plain white belt after many examinations of his technique and expertise. It is not because he now knows everything about his field, rather that his experience and acquired wisdom serves to show him how little he really knows. It is only by becoming expert that you will find out how much expertise there still remains to gain.

Baking artisan bread is just the same. It's a constant learning curve. When I first started I was making my own bread in a bowl at home, as many of the readers of this book will be doing. I learned a bit more and developed some better technique as I started to supply friends and family with bread on a regular basis. When I turned professional full-time I scaled the mixes up quite dramatically and developed new strategies and ways of dealing with the dough to make the bread better. But it is now, when I have maybe thirty years of experience, that I realise how little I really know and how vast is the untapped seam of possibility out there waiting for me.

I suppose that the first challenge for you is to define even vaguely what you consider to be excellence. I find much of the supposedly excellent mass-produced fake 'artisan bread' in the industry to be utterly abhorrent. I'm thinking that most lovers of Real Bread would agree with me.

Pallid bone-white 'crumb' with a pale ochre papery artificial-looking crust just doesn't say 'artisan made' for me. I want the jagged irregular crust of the real thing, with its varied colours and the odd unintended split in the oven. These latter examples are so much more interesting both to look at and to eat, as the texture of crust and crumb will change three or four times within the loaf as you eat it. I don't want uniform; certainly not if it comes at the cost of flavour and texture.

Your own pursuit of excellence is unlikely to be greatly assisted by the purchase of loads of high-tech professional kit either. You will find as you improve your technique your bread will improve in equal measure. It does depend also upon which path you choose for your experiments. If your aspiration is to produce the perfect *baguette à l'Ancienne* then you are going to need a little capital investment. The best baguettes and flûtes I've eaten have all come from the hearth of a big wood-fired oven complete with steam injectors. The steam allows the dough a little bit more spring in the oven, which makes for a lighter, crisper crust and a great open texture in the bread. The downside of this type of equipment is that it

will cost a substantial amount of money. Fine if you are intent on opening your own bakery full-time, but hard to reconcile with home breadmaking. It is easy to overstretch the budget but wiser perhaps to limit your ambition to a more achievable goal.

Also a factor to consider is where you want to draw your satisfaction from - whether you are seeking general enthusiastic applause from an audience who know little about food, or detailed critique from foodies with a more educated palate, who can detect the differences of taste and texture. At the end of the quest, this may not be enough, and you will need to seek out tasters who, like you, are dedicated to real artisan bread. Artisan bakers are the most educated and helpful critics of your baking because they know what you are trying to do and appreciate the journey you are on. In fact you are on the same journey although other bakers are far ahead or just behind you.

For me, the first group and the last are the most rewarding. The general audience reaction is the most dramatic, although not always in a good way! They will give an honest opinion of your efforts and every now and then you will change someone's life. Worth it, every time.

The foodies, it often seems, are too on-trend to give an objective opinion. Many of them want to appear sophisticated, so will find something to complain about because they do not understand what is required of a critic. Their opinions are occasionally interesting, regularly ludicrous and never ever to be relied upon as a guide to your progress. As you improve and go 'off piste' more frequently, their lack of understanding will become more apparent.

Real artisan bakers are your peer group, even if you bake rarely. They understand your need to do what you do. They know what is a genuine fault, and what is an experiment. They recognise the taste of too much yeast or salt. Above all, they will give you an honest opinion of your bread in terms of taste, texture, technique, crust, crumb, and grains.

In my experience, real artisan bakers are generally supportive and helpful when asked for advice, and are happy to be consulted by another enthusiast. This is my favourite focus group. I know many exceptional real artisan bakers, not all of them professionals. I value their opinion because I know they produce bread that I would be proud to have made myself, and because I am as happy to eat their bread as my own. There are some professional artisan bakers whose opinion I would not ask for. I do not consider that they are competent to judge the real thing if their own efforts are a poor apology for the genuine article.

Only you know what you are trying to achieve and which specific excellence you are in pursuit of.

When you consider it logically, the best-qualified person to judge your bread is you yourself. Only you know what you are trying to achieve and which specific excellence you are in pursuit of. It is a very individual judgment. Personally, I like really heavyweight, seedy multigrain loaves with a thick chewy crust and loads of earthy flavours. That might be your idea of hell on earth as you strive for the perfect light-as-air croissant or super-rich golden brioche. Lots of people hate these sorts of bread and that is fair enough too. They are allowed to hate it but as long as I can carry on baking and eating my own style of Real Bread I'm happy.

Three Day Multigrain

This is probably the most ancient of breadmaking techniques and paradoxically both the simplest and the most complicated. The principle is one well worth mastering, as it allows you to make bread with a much wider range of grains, flours and seeds. The flavours have lots of time to develop so you can expect breads full of earthy tastes and a chewy texture.

 This one also keeps exceptionally well, and even when stale it is still usable to make crackers for cheese.

Method

Three days before baking, put all the dry ingredients for the soaker into a large bowl or a plastic pail. Bring the milk to the boil and pour over the grains. Add the oil and coffee and stir well to combine all the ingredients. Cover the top and leave at room temperature for two hours, then stir well to break up any clumps that have formed

 If the soaker appears dry, add another 100ml boiling water. Cover for three days, stirring once or twice. The mix should have the texture of thick porridge.

 On day three, combine the flour, yeast and salt in a bowl and make a well in the centre. Add the entire soaker and mix well, adding warm water as required to create a soft, pliable dough. Cover the bowl. Prove for two hours in a warm place.

 Grease three 2lb bread tins. Turn the dough out onto flour. Knead briefly and divide into three.

 Shape into ovals and rise in tins for two hours.

Heat the oven to 190°C.

Ingredients

For the soaker

50g wheat grain boiled for 15 minutes

50g oats

50g oat or wheat bran

50g rye flakes

50g barley/quinoa/spelt flakes

1 teaspoon caraway seeds

50g golden linseed

5g coriander seeds, broken

80ml espresso coffee

80ml vegetable oil

400ml boiling whole milk

For the dough

1.5kg wholemeal breadmaking flour

2 teaspoons Fermipan dried yeast

3 teaspoons salt

Glaze the loaves with egg white and scatter with seeds if you like. Slash each loaf once down the middle and bake in the centre of the oven for five minutes, then turn the oven to 170°C.

Test after 45 minutes. Cool on a wire rack when baked.

Enjoy with cheeses, charcuterie or just butter.

If you prefer, you could make this with sourdough rather than bakers' yeast. If you do decide to do it this way, be aware that the sourdough flavours will be enhanced by the mature soaker and it may be a little more acidic than usual.

To make crackers from any leftovers of this loaf is easy and well worth trying out, even if it does break your heart to let the bread stale deliberately!

Soak thin slices of bread briefly in cold water and then roll out to a thickness of 1-2mm with a rolling pin. If you want uniform shapes use a pastry cutter to stamp them out, otherwise just transfer the pieces to a baking sheet and bake in a very slow (100°C) oven for two hours. Leave the trays in with the door open until the oven is cold. Store in an airtight box for up to two weeks and serve with butter and cheeses, or with pâté as a substitute for the ubiquitous Melba toast.

Bagels

Or beigels perhaps? Most sources seem to agree that bagels are of Eastern European origin but there is no doubt that this is the bread which brings to mind the USA more than any other. New Yorkers are prepared to argue for hours over the relative merits of bagel bakeries and their different flavours and toppings.

However London boasts several fabulous bagel bakeries including the celebrated Beigel Bake on Brick Lane. This testament to the Jewish baking tradition is open round the clock and still manages to produce some of the best bagels you will ever taste, as well as perfect challah. The joy of biting into a properly-baked bagel makes me realise how very poor are the factory variety available from a multitude of high street outlets, with their tough leathery skins and dry, charmless crumb.

Make these once and your friends and family will talk about them for weeks! Be warned, you may create a monster. Fresh bagels are so good that they become addictive.

Method

Mix the dry ingredients in a bowl and make a well in the centre. Dissolve the honey or malt in 200ml of the warm water and add to the bowl. Mix, adding more water as needed until you have a firm but pliable dough.

Cover the bowl with clingfilm and rise in a warm place for two hours.

Heat oven to 200°C and grease two baking sheets.

Turn the risen dough out onto a well-floured surface and knead briefly. Divide into 50g pieces and shape into rolls. When all are done, push your thumbs through the centre of each one to make the hole, stretching it open to 8cm diameter. Set each one aside on a floured tray. Bring a large pan of water and malt extract to a rolling boil and poach each bagel for two minutes each side. Lift them out with a slotted spoon and transfer to a baking sheet.

Brush with eggwash and sprinkle with seeds if you like. Sesame or poppy are traditional.

Bake for 25 minutes. The bagels should be firm and golden brown. Cool on a wire rack.

Once cold, bagels make great sandwiches; the classic is smoked salmon with cream cheese. They toast perfectly, and are especially delicious topped with creamy scrambled eggs and chives. Bagels will freeze well for up to a month.

Ingredients

1kg strong white breadmaking flour

1 teaspoon dry / 15g fresh yeast

Half a teaspoon salt

1 tablespoon honey or malt extract

650ml warm water

Eggwash and poppy or sesame seeds if liked

3 litres boiling water

2 tablespoons malt extract for kettling

Tsoureki for Kendal Festival of Food

Easter breads tend to be luxurious, often containing extravagant quantities of rich and expensive ingredients. Eggs are seasonably ubiquitous and exotic spices and preserved fruits abound. The one which struck me as a wonderful bread for breakfast on Easter Sunday was from Greece, a country whose breadmaking tradition dates back thousands of years. For the Greek bakers every Orthodox religious festival merits its own special bread and Easter is just as important as Christmas so the breads are correspondingly spectacular.
I'm not claiming any particular authenticity for this recipe, but it does work well. I have left the recipe as simple as possible to make it easier but equally spectacular. The ingredients are easily available too and you could get the children involved in colouring the eggs. Make sure you use edible food colourings though!

Method

Colour 600ml of water with enough red food colouring to make a dark red solution. Boil four eggs for seven minutes and put them on a rack to dry. They should be a nice pink hue. When dry, rub them over with a little olive oil to fix. Leave to dry thoroughly.

Dissolve the yeast in the warm milk and whisk in a handful of the flour. Cover and set aside for 15 mins.

Combine all the dry ingredients in a bowl and add the butter. Make a well in the centre and add the eggs with the yeast mixture. Mix well until you have a soft pliable dough. It's fine if it is a bit sticky.

Cover the bowl with clingfilm or a clean dry tea towel and prove in a warm place for three hours.

Turn out onto a well-floured surface and knead gently until it becomes a smooth elastic dough. Shape into a long narrow rectangle and divide in three lengthwise. Plait the three strands together loosely and put on a greased baking sheet.

Make the glaze by dissolving the honey in hot water and allow it to cool a little before beating in the egg. Glaze the loaf and set somewhere warm to rise for 90 minutes. Heat the oven to 190°C.

Glaze the loaf again and insert the eggs into the hollows formed by the intersections of the plait. Sprinkle with slivered almonds and bake in the centre of the oven for 40 mins, turning the oven down to 170°C after ten minutes. This is a big loaf, so you may need to turn it once during baking to ensure an even colour and texture.

Test the loaf by tapping the base and return to the oven for five to ten minutes if not done.

Cool on a wire rack and enjoy with creamy cheeses or with good butter. The hard-boiled and baked eggs are great for sandwich filling with a little mayonnaise, snipped chives and some ground black pepper.

Ingredients

For the dough

500g strong white bread flour

1 teaspoon salt

1 teaspoon fennel seeds or aniseed

1 teaspoon ground allspice

1 teaspoon ground cinnamon

A pinch of grated nutmeg

3 tablespoons caster sugar

50g chopped blanched almonds (optional)

50g finely chopped candied orange peel
(optional)

80g unsalted butter, cubed

3 large eggs, beaten

200ml warm full fat milk

2 teaspoons dried yeast or 30g fresh yeast

For the eggs

Red or pink edible food colouring

4 hard-boiled eggs

1 teaspoon olive oil

For the glaze

1 egg yolk

1 teaspoon honey

1 teaspoon hot water

To finish

30g flaked blanched almonds

Spring Buckwheat Bread

Usually one comes across buckwheat in pancakes or blinis, where the grey colour with its darker flecks is very obvious. In this loaf the buckwheat is indistinct but the flavour is definitely there, along with a delicious chewy crumb and astonishing keeping qualities. I chose this bread to try out my new handmill. It works best when the wheat and the buckwheat are ground into flour together. You can do this at home in a coffee mill or a spice grinder. Whole wheat grain and whole buckwheat are both available from your local wholefood shop. This bread is worth making for the slight roasted bitterness of the buckwheat which blends so well with the rich flavours of the whole wheat flour. Try it with homemade leek soup – the perfect combination.

Method

Blend the dry ingredients together in a large bowl, making a well in the centre. Mix the beaten eggs with the oil and the milk and add to the flour mix along with half the water. Mix by hand to form a slightly sticky dough, adding more water as necessary.

Cover the bowl with clingfilm and prove somewhere warm for four hours. Turn out the dough onto a floured surface and knead gently until it is pliable and elastic, then divide it in two and again knead each half. Shape each into a long oval, place on a greased baking sheet and cover with oiled clingfilm. Prove in a warm place for 45 minutes. Heat the oven to 180°C. Brush the loaves with a little eggwash and slash once lengthwise. Bake for 40 minutes. Cool on a wire rack.

This bread is ideal for a larder-foraged lunch with some cheese, pâté or cold cuts from the fridge and a glass of craft IPA beer.

Feel free to vary the proportions of buckwheat to wheat in the recipe but remember that buckwheat is not a wheat and has no gluten. This does affect its ability to make a good crumb, so unless you want a very dense loaf indeed I would stick to 20 per cent buckwheat or less as a percentage of the total flour used.

Ingredients

500g wholemeal breadmaking flour

75g buckwheat flour

(buy as whole grain and mill together if possible, otherwise blend flours together)

125g strong white bread flour

8g salt

20g caraway seeds (optional)

10g crushed coriander seeds

1.5 teaspoons Fermipan dried yeast (or 20g fresh)

2 large eggs

200ml soured milk or buttermilk

2 tablespoons rapeseed oil

200ml warm water

(100ml extra warm water as required)

My Version of Black Bread. Mk I

Method for the soaker

Slice the bread thinly and toast until very dark brown and thoroughly dried out. Allow to cool and crumble into a large bowl. Add the other ingredients and stir well. Make 250ml of strong coffee and dissolve the molasses in it, then pour over the soaker. Cover the bowl with a lid or plastic wrap and leave to absorb the liquid for two hours. Add another 100ml of boiling water to the soaker and re-cover. Leave overnight. In the morning check the consistency; it should still be moist. If not, add 50ml of boiling water and re-cover for 2-3 hours.

Method for the dough

Mix the flours, yeast and salt in a bowl. Add all the soaker and mix until you have formed a slightly sticky dough, using the extra water as necessary. This dough will not absorb as much water as usual due to the amount already in the soaker, so take care as you are mixing not to over-hydrate it. Cover and set to rise at room temperature for 3-4 hours. Turn out onto a floured board and knead. You may need to add extra flour if the dough is very sticky. This dough will make three loaves and bakes particularly well in a tin. You can bake it on a greased tray if you prefer. Allow the loaves to rise for one hour at room temperature. Heat the oven to 200°C. Slash the top of the loaves a couple of times and bake at 180°C for 40 minutes before checking to see if they are done. Cool on a wire rack.

Black breads are perfect for rustic bread and cheese lunches but the complex flavours also make it a sophisticated partner for soft and semi-soft cheese boards. It keeps very well and freezes well for up to three months if wrapped in plastic and well sealed.

Ingredients

For the soaker

100g dark rye or wholemeal bread

25g golden linseeds

25g cracked wheat

25g buckwheat

25g rye or quinoa flakes

10g caraway seeds

2 tablespoons olive or vegetable oil

Coffee - real or instant as you please

2 tablespoons molasses or black treacle

For the dough

350g white breadmaking flour

150g wholemeal or rye flour, or a mixture of the two

10g salt

1 teaspoon dried yeast (or 2 cups sourdough starter)

150ml warm water

My Version of Black Bread. Mk II

Method for the soaker

Stir all the dry ingredients together in a large bowl and then add the water. Stir briefly then cover for three hours. Add another 100ml boiling water and set aside, covered for at least eight hours or overnight.

Method for the dough

Mix all the dry ingredients together then add the soaker and the milk. Mix until you have a sticky dough using the warm water as necessary. Turn it out onto a floured board and knead it briefly to ensure that the dough is not too wet, then put back in the bowl and cover. Rise at room temperature for at least six hours or in a cool place, overnight. Turn out onto a floured board and divide into three small or two medium loaves. Knead until toned then place on a greased baking sheet. Allow to rise for one hour. Heat the oven to 220°C. Brush the crust with milk and slash with a sharp blade. Turn the oven down to 190°C and bake in the centre for 45 minutes. Cool on a wire rack.

This second version is creamier and a little softer but with less fat. The cardamon makes it slightly exotic too. Great for cheese on toast or the more sophisticated rarebit. A lovely long-lasting loaf which toasts beautifully too.

Ingredients

For the soaker

100g dark rye or wholemeal bread, toasted until very dark brown and thoroughly dry

25g cracked rye

25g cracked wheat

25g barley flakes

25g jumbo oats

10g poppy seeds, lightly toasted

10g sesame seeds, lightly toasted

10g cardamom seeds, crushed

1 tablespoon cocoa powder

2 tablespoons molasses or black treacle

1 tablespoon instant coffee powder

200ml boiling water

For the dough

500g white breadmaking flour

18g salt

1 teaspoon dried yeast (or 2 cups of sourdough starter)

100ml whole milk, warmed

100ml warm water

Pain (*Extra-*) Ordinaire

This recipe uses the system of *pâte fermentée*, to add taste and complexity and a better texture to what is essentially a plain white loaf. To make this recipe you will need to reserve a walnut-sized piece of dough from your last batch of white bread. It will keep in the fridge for a couple of days if you cover it with clingfilm, but should at any rate be kept for 24 hours before making this recipe.

Method

Combine the dry ingredients in a bowl. Tear or cut the reserved dough into small pieces and disperse throughout the flour. Make a well in the centre and mix in the water gradually until you have a firm but smooth dough. Cover the bowl and rise in a warm place for two hours. Turn out onto a floured surface and knead briefly. The dough should feel pliable but fairly firm. Cut the dough in half and knead one half into a long oval loaf. Set to rise on a baking sheet or rise in a floured basket if you intend to bake on a stone or the oven hearth. Divide the other half of the dough into two or three pieces, depending on whether you intend large or small flûtes. Knead the pieces into small ovals and set aside to rest for 10 minutes. Heat the oven to 220ºC and put the baking stone in if using one. Place a linen tea towel on a tray and dust with flour. Set aside. On a lightly floured board take one oval of dough and press across the long axis with your finger to make a crease. It should look like a coffee bean. Fold the oval down the crease and seal the edge by crimping with your fingertips.

Ingredients

500g white breadmaking flour

1 teaspoon dried yeast

8g salt

1 walnut-sized piece of reserved dough from a previous batch

300ml warm water

150ml warm water

It should now resemble a Cornish pasty. Turn the dough through 180 degrees. Now, working from right to left, push your left thumbtip into the edge of the "pasty" and fold the dough over it with your right hand, sealing the edge as you go with your right thumb. When you have folded it the whole way along the side, repeat the same again. Twice. This step sounds much more complicated than it is and you will soon build up speed and confidence. Look at the photographs for help in understanding what is needed. Once you have finished this folding and sealing you will notice that the roll is now looking decidedly more flûte-like. A good thickness to aim for is about 2cm. Begin rolling the cylinder with your hands lightly floured. Start at the centre and work outwards. Spread your fingers and move gradually towards the ends, trying to keep the thickness even. When you feel the end of the flûte between your third and fourth finger, press down hard and at the same time turn your hand up to 45 degrees to the tabletop. This will cause the tip of the flûte to catch between the edge of your hand and the table, then as you roll the dough forward the friction will shape the tip into a point. It sounds more complicated than it really is, so persevere and you will soon be producing suitably hazardous points to your *flûtes artisans*. It is the point that makes them so impressive to the uninitiated. Without it, they are still superb French flûtes.

The traditional method of proving these flûtes and also their larger siblings, baguettes, is in a couche. This is just a square of linen, floured and pleated to hold the sticks of dough whilst they rise. A linen tea towel or a tablecloth is perfect for this purpose. Lay

the cloth out on a flat tray or on your worktop and dust it with flour. When your first flûte is shaped lay it about 5cm from the edge of the cloth and pinch the linen up into a fence on either side of it, so that the flûte lies in a "furrow" of floured cloth. You should place a rolling pin or a baton at the edge of the couche to support the fence. The next flûte should lie alongside the first, with the cloth pinched up again to make the next fence. The last one will need some support too so that the structure resembles a corrugated sheet with the loaves in the furrows. Cover the whole sheet with a tea towel and leave it for 20-30 minutes. The flûtes should rise quickly and evenly. To transfer them to the bakestone it is probably best to use a flat metal baking sheet slightly longer than the flûtes. Dust the baking sheet lightly with a little polenta or semolina and gently roll the flûte from the

linen over onto it. Make five or six cuts at 45 degrees along the top and transfer to the stone. Try and keep the flûte the right way up as you slide it onto the stone. It is probably wise to bake the flûtes two or three at a time as they bake quite quickly: 20-25 minutes dependent on their size. They will turn light brown when ready and you will be able to remove them from the oven with oven gloves. Cool them on a rack, or, if you have a double oven, cool on the shelf of a barely warm oven for ten minutes before transferring to the wire rack. Flûtes are moments of bliss and should be eaten fairly shortly after baking. The next day they are usable as pizza base but after that they are fit only for croutons or crumbs so resist the temptation to make lots. Use most of the dough for *Pain Ordinaire* and make only two or three flûtes as a treat.

Walnut Bread

Method

Combine the dry ingredients in a bowl and make a well in the centre. Add the butter and walnut oil (and honey if using) and then the warm milk. Mix into the flour, adding more water as needed. The mix should come together quickly into a smooth dough. Chances are that you will not need all the water to achieve a nice smooth dough. Set the bowl aside for 10-15 minutes and check hydration. Cover and prove in a warm place for three hours or halve the yeast and rise at room temperature for 12 hours. Turn out onto a floured board and knead gently until 'toned'. Divide in two and knead each piece into a round loaf. Put on an oiled baking sheet and set to rise for one hour in a warm draught-free place. Heat the oven to 220°C. Brush the crusts gently with one egg yolk beaten with two teaspoons of cold water. Slash the crust with a sharp blade. Transfer to the centre of the oven turn down to 180°C and bake for 35 minutes. The crust should be deep mahogany brown and shiny. If not cooked through return to the oven for up to another 10 minutes. Cool on a wire rack.

The richness of the walnut oil, milk and butter make this the perfect loaf for keeping, freezing (up to three months) and toasting. Its slightly mauve colour, from the walnut skins, makes it visually appealing as a sandwich too. It works particularly well with rich blue cheeses and with ham as a sandwich. The texture is smooth, punctuated by the crunch of the walnuts.

As a variation you can add fruit. Golden raisins work very well. Use about 60g. Bear in mind that you may need to increase the liquid accordingly.

Ingredients

600g white breadmaking flour

8g salt

1 teapoon active dried yeast Fermipan

100g light amber walnuts

(the lighter skinned ones taste less bitter)

(1 tablespoon honey if you intend a sweet loaf)

25g unsalted butter

2 tablespoons walnut oil

300ml whole milk, warmed

150ml warm water

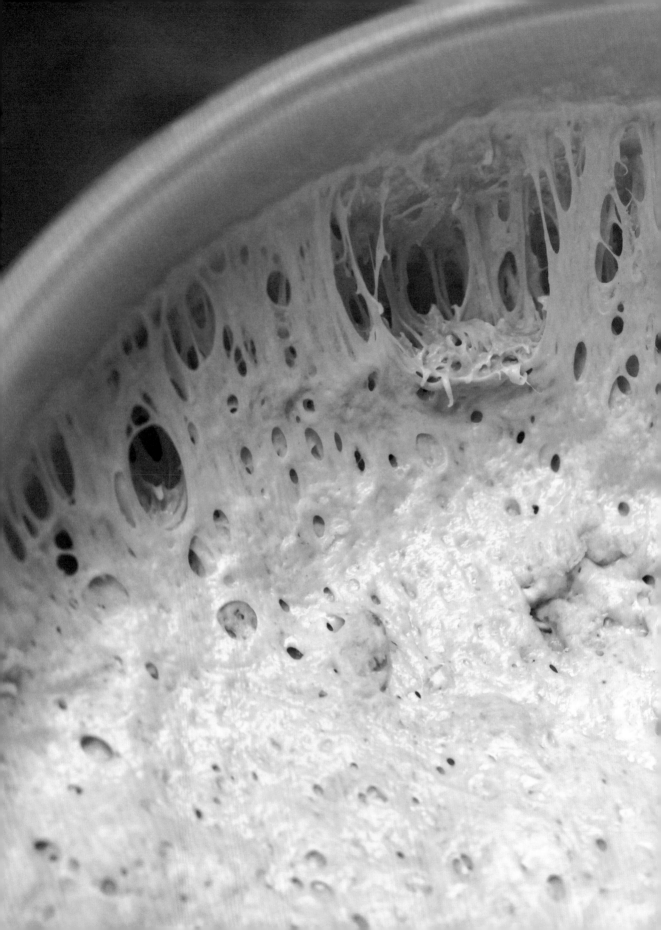

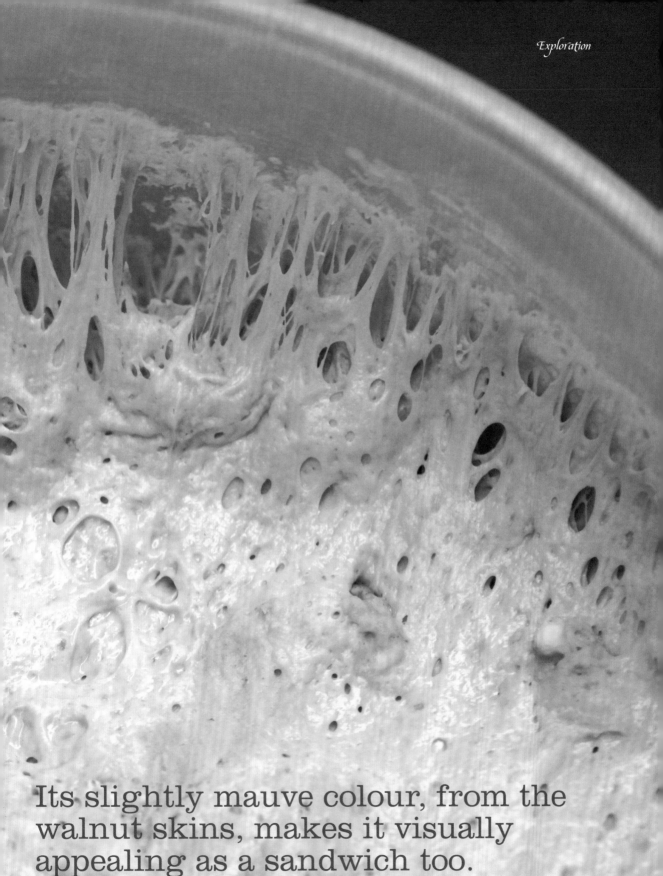

Its slightly mauve colour, from the walnut skins, makes it visually appealing as a sandwich too.

Play: The Pursuit of Fun

Most recipes, by their very nature, tend to be fairly strictly defined. "Thou shalt use 500g of flour" et cetera. This is fine for many readers and occasions when what is required is a formula to produce a facsimile of the original dish. My approach to Real Artisan Bread is slightly different in that there is a basic technique to master and a definite product to finish up with. But within that framework there is scope for all sorts of entertaining variation and individuality.

For example, if your vision of ultimate sophistication in baking is a bacon sandwich, you may want to try baking the bread with the bacon already inside it before baking. If you use a thin layer of dough to wrap around the part-cooked bacon then fold and seal the edges, you have a bacon sandwich which can be baked in the oven.

Does it work? I have no idea as I've never been that keen to find out. In theory it should. In practice it may not. You could have some fun finding out though. For example, in Portugal there is a delicious bread called *pão com chouriço* which is their equivalent of a sausage roll. It's literally a torpedo-shaped bread roll with a whole *chouriço* sausage baked in the middle of it. They are excellent as street food or for picnics. That should prove that there is no reason not to try out your theories.

History will show you that almost anything which can be baked in a pastry shell can also be baked in a bread. Before there was pastry everything was baked wrapped in bread dough. I have a recipe for baking a fillet of beef wrapped in bread dough which dates back to the Middle Ages. It predates *boeuf en croûte* and beef Wellington by four or five hundred years.

There are a couple of traditional breads in

Brittany with fish baked in them and the Russians have *coulibiac*, a delicious baked fish pie using bread dough rather than pastry. Bread dough is much more tolerant to variations in the oven than pastry and in the past it would be easily and universally available. Even if you didn't have any dough yourself on a non-baking day there would be a neighbour or a local baker who would supply some for a pie.

If you want to bake bread with chocolate chips in it, that's great. Why not? *Pain au chocolat* is a highlight of visits to France. It is indeed made with a bread dough, albeit augmented with a ton of butter so that it resembles puff pastry. Have a go - it's fun. My favourite recipe is in the Michel Roux OBE classic book on pastry. I'm not going to reproduce it here because you should own that book. It is simply brilliant and inspirational.

Once you have tried classic *pain au chocolat* you should think about moving on. Try swapping your usual laminated croissant dough for a light milk dough. Trade your usual plain chocolate for a variation containing sea salt or chilli perhaps. Introduce some traditional South American *xocolatl* spice notes or use a Mexican '*mole*' recipe to make a savoury chocolate bread.

Once you step away from the recipe a little and start to think about might be possible you will realise that you are on the bottom rung of an infinite ladder. Each step is a learning experience and, for better or worse, it will help you improve your understanding and technique.

You will become familiar with the basic techniques and understand the principles which introduce gases into the dough to make bread lighter and more open-textured. You will remember the effect of sugars on the dough, making the rise quicker, and the citrus fruits which accelerate fermentation and bring a silky smoothness to the dough. When these things are integral to recipe planning you will be able to bring new factors to bear and introduce new ingredients to the mix. Some might call it messing about with the recipe, but they are the bakers of limited imagination and ambition. They will get comments from tasters like "that's nice" but yours will be

"wow! that's awesome". I know which reaction I prefer.

Making staggeringly good Real Artisan Bread is a question of experimentation and development. When you get a result you're happy with and proud of then share it with your friends and family. Nurture and develop the basic recipe until you are satisfied that it is as good as it can possibly be.

If you are not happy with the result of an experiment you can often still eat it or just bin it!! There have been very occasional things which we have binned over the years which have been nowhere near what I was expecting. I once made a bread dough with pickled onions baked in it. A reasonable enough idea, I thought, but the result was absolutely vile. The next step in its evolution was a sourdough boule with sauerkraut in which was delicious.

Artisan baking is a licence to be more interesting with your bread repertoire. So try it.

Carlton Focaccia

Focaccia is always the first thing my students learn to make on a real bread course at the bakery or at the lovely Carlton Towers Cooks courses. It's a very wet dough and has no salt or sugar in it, so is a good opportunity to step outside the comfort zone of home breadmaking and learn something really new. It is always the recipe which everyone remembers and I often see it reproduced in leaflets and on social media.

This recipe can be used not only for focaccia but also as a pizza base as well.

Method

Mix the flour and yeast in a large bowl and make a well in the centre. Add the olive oil and then pour on a third of the water. Mix in the water and add more as required to make a smooth very wet dough with no lumps. It helps to squeeze the dough through your fingers to remove the lumps. When it is finished, the dough should have the consistency of lightly-whipped cream - still pourable but not liquid.

Cover the bowl with clingfilm and prove for one to two hours in a warm place. It should be frothy with loads of bubbles.

Turn out onto a well-floured board and work a little flour into it with a scraper by folding the outside to the centre repeatedly and rolling the dough from one end of the floured board to the other. Add more sieved flour as necessary until the wet dough can be handled with care and transferred to a parchment-lined baking sheet.

It is important not to try and grip the dough with your fingers but rather to support it and lift with flat hands and possibly forearms too. This will allow you to handle the dough without adding too much extra flour and losing the unique texture of this loaf.

When you have transferred the dough to the baking tray, fill your empty dough bowl with cold water and thoroughly wash your hands to remove any dried dough stuck to them.

With dripping wet hands, press the dough

Ingredients

300g strong white bread flour

1 teaspoon Fermipan dried yeast / 0.5oz fresh yeast

4 tablespoons extra virgin olive oil plus extra for drizzling

220ml warm water (you may not need quite all of it)

Plus another 100g flour to knead with

1 dessertspoon coarse sea salt flakes

out to a thickness of about 1.5cm. As soon as your hands start to stick to the dough, dip them back into the water again. As long as they are dripping wet they won't stick to the wet dough. It sounds counter-intuitive but believe me, it works. Dimple the surface of the dough by pressing down hard with your wet fingertips, then drizzle with olive oil, sprinkle with dried rosemary and add a few pinches of coarse sea salt.

Bake at 220°C for 20 minutes or until golden brown. Have a peep under the focaccia to check that the bottom is cooked. Cool on a wire rack until warm, then serve with a big bowl of fresh ripe tomatoes, marinated olives and some cheeses and charcuterie. Fast food doesn't have to taste like carpet underlay. This is easy to put together in a short time and is guaranteed to impress.

If you want to push the boat out with some grilled chicken, capers, tomato, romaine lettuce and prosciutto, it makes great club sandwiches too.

The finished focaccia makes a great base for those French bread pizzas, better known as cheese on toast, up to three or four days after baking.

If you want to make genuine pizza just reserve 100g of dough for each 25cm pizza base. Chill the dough in the fridge overnight and it will develop flavour and become stronger structurally.

When you are ready to make your pizzaolo sauce, take the dough from the fridge and bring it to room temperature before giving it a light knead and a short rest. Stretch the dough by hand rather than rolling with a pin – it gives a better texture to the baked pizza.

Bath Buns

Certainly the Bath bun is associated these days with the city of Bath down in the West of England but its origins are slightly obscure. For a baker, this peculiarly scruffy-looking pile of dough, fruit and sugar looks very strange and unformed.

The joy of it is, to some extent at least, found in the anarchy of its shape - a uniform standard Bath bun would merely be a fruit bun. But these heaps of loveliness just scream "Eat me!" For many people it evokes childhood memories so I present it as a perfect comfort food.

Method

Mix the yeast, sugar, beaten eggs, 50g of the flour and 250ml warm water in a bowl. Stir the lemon juice into the sultanas and lemon peel in another. Cover both and set in a warm place for one hour.

Blend the remaining flour, butter and salt in a bowl. Make a well in the centre and add the yeast mixture then the fruit. Mix well, adding more water as needed to achieve a smooth dough. Cover and prove in a warm place for two hours, then tear the dough and incorporate the sugar nibs if using. Prove for 30 minutes then turn out the dough and divide into 60g pieces.

Don't knead them: they are meant to look scruffy. Just gather the dough into small heaps and cut it several times with a dough scraper so it doesn't rise as a round bun. Butter a baking sheet and place the buns 5cm apart. Prove for 90 minutes in a warm place then brush with eggwash and scatter with sugar nibs. Batch bake at 200°C for 20-25 minutes. Cool on a wire rack and enjoy them with or without butter. Anything else in the way of toppings is overkill.

Ingredients

650g strong white bread flour

25g caster sugar

3 teaspoons Fermipan dried yeast (40g fresh)

6 large free range eggs (plus one more for eggwash)

250ml lukewarm water

200g butter

Half a teaspoon salt

2 tablespoons lemon juice

60g cut candied lemon peel

120g good sultanas

55ml warm water as necessary

Optional but authentic: 150g sugar nibs

(available online or from specialist bakers' suppliers)

Glacé cherries are often included but are not traditional. If you do put them in, use 60g and reduce the sultanas by 40g. Leave them in big pieces - nothing smaller than a quarter is acceptable.

Breadsticks? Or Stickbreads?

Italian grissini were the starting point for this recipe, but the final result is more like a real bread than the desiccated sticks found on the tables of many of the poorer Anglo-Italian restaurants. Make them while the children are off school as they will enjoy helping, and eating too.

Method

Mix the dry ingredients in a large bowl and make a well in the centre. Pour in the oil and one-third of the water. Mix slowly, adding more water as required to achieve a slightly sticky soft dough.

Cover the bowl with clingfilm and prove in a warm place for two hours.

Line two large cookie sheets with parchment.

Turn the dough out onto a thin bed of flour and knead until the dough is firm but still pliant. Divide the dough into 30g pieces and knead each piece into a ball. Set aside on a little flour until all are done. Beginning with the first one you kneaded, roll each one from the centre to form a stick about 1cm thick. Transfer them to the baking sheet as you complete each one. Set them 2cm apart to allow for expansion. Prove for one hour in a warm place.

Heat the oven to 200°C.

Bake the breadsticks in the centre of the oven for 20-25 minutes.

When they are ready, the breadsticks should be golden brown and firm to the touch. The crust will soften slightly as they cool due to the olive oil in the dough.

Ingredients

1kg strong white breadmaking flour

10g fine salt

1 teaspoon dried or 15g fresh yeast

2 tablespoons extra virgin olive oil, rapeseed oil or sunflower oil

600ml warm water

Extra flour for kneading

Cool on a wire rack.

Feel free to play with this recipe by adding flavours to the initial dough: chilli oil, herbs and spices. It does work best with white flour rather than wholemeal, but you can use a little (ten per cent or so) polenta to add some extra crunch. You can also coat them with black or white (or both) sesame seeds or poppy seeds by glazing the sticks with beaten egg white and sprinkling with seeds before baking.

These are just perfect for entertaining both children and adults and a relatively modest batch will produce plenty for even a large gathering.

Serve for dipping with hummus, salsa etc. For a change, treat them as if they are miniature baguettes. They can easily be split, buttered and filled to make tiny sandwiches for children or fun canapés for parties. Cut them into 1cm thick slices diagonally and you will have a tray full of miniature crostini in no time by just chopping a few ripe tomatoes and some fresh herbs. Spoon onto the bread and finish with a twist of black pepper and a drop of olive oil.

My own favourite is to split them and fill with Cumberland Farmhouse cheese, wrap each in Woodalls air-dried ham and put under a hot grill for two minutes. That's my desert island luxury, hot or cold.

Simply Seedy Flatbreads

These are so easy to make and are very popular at picnics or as a tasty snack with olives and drinks. We often make them at home for dips and hummus. They don't freeze but if dried out in the oven they will last a week in an airtight box while you optimistically wait for the sunshine!

Method

Heat a heavy frying pan and toast the seeds until they start to sizzle and pop. Pour the Worcestershire sauce onto the seeds and remove the pan from the heat. Stir to coat them and set aside to cool.

Smoked Spanish paprika, or *pimentón de la vera*, comes in rather pretty tins and is often just left to languish as a kitchen ornament for those who don't know what to do with it. There are three variants: sweet or *'dulce'*, hot or *'picante'*, and bittersweet or *'agridulce'*. All of them are delicious as a condiment, in tapas dishes and in casseroled and stewed meat dishes. They also make a great coating for roasted nuts as a cocktail snack. If you are using different *pimentón* varieties, split the seeds into equal portions and season each with salt and a single *pimentón*.

Brush one side of the bread with melted butter and put it onto a baking sheet, butter side down.

Brush the top of each slice with egg white and sprinkle half of them liberally with seed mixture. Put the un-sprinkled slices on top to make a sandwich and cover with baking parchment. Place another baking sheet on top and press the sandwiches together with weights for at least an hour.

Heat the oven to 180°C. Uncover the 'sandwiches', which should now be flattened to about 4mm. Bake the flatbreads for ten minutes, then turn them over for another ten. Turn the oven off, open the door and leave them in until the oven is cold. When they look like toast, move them to a cooling rack.

Serve warm with hummus, guacamole, cream cheese or cold with pâtés and cheeseboards.

Ingredients

1 large white or wholemeal loaf sliced into pieces 5mm thick

200g unsalted butter, melted

3 egg whites, beaten with 1 teaspoon cold water

1 dessert teaspoon flaky sea salt like Maldon

400g mixed seeds (pumpkin, sesame, black sesame, poppy, etc)

Pimentón Spanish paprika (ideally all three varieties)

1 tablespoon Worcestershire sauce

Spotted Dog

This recipe is not what I'd really call Real Bread but it is very tasty and very, very quick to make. So I'm putting it in for those times when you want a nice fruitbread to toast for breakfast or a different bread to complement your cheeseboard after dinner. It's also perfect for children to make as they can eat it almost immediately. Technically it's a soda bread and probably Irish in origin but it came to me from the North-East of England via Grandma Thomas.

Method

Grease two 1lb loaf tins or one baking tray. Pre-heat the oven to 220°C. Mix the dry ingredients in a bowl and make a well in the centre. Whisk the treacle into the buttermilk and pour it in. Add the raisins with their liquid and mix well with a spoon to form a sticky dough. Turn out onto a bed of flour and fold it together to form a ball. If using tins, divide in two, shape into an oval and drop in tins. Otherwise put the ball of dough on a baking tray and flatten to about 4cm thick.

  Cut deeply to make a cross on the loaf. Brush with milk and put in the oven for five minutes, then reduce temperature to 180°C for another 25 minutes before testing the loaf by knocking on the bottom. The done loaf should sound resonant. If it isn't done, put it back in the oven for another five minutes.

  Cool on a wire rack and enjoy with butter, jam or mature cheeses. You can vary this recipe by using other dried fruits like apple or apricot. If you want to have it with cheeses, the addition of one teaspoon of caraway seeds makes a pleasant change too.

Unlike 'real bread,' soda breads are not good keepers, and become stale quickly. If you want to eat it without toasting, it is best made on the day you need it. Allow the loaf to cool on a wire rack and then wrap it in a clean tea towel at room temperature until you need it.

Ingredients

(Makes 2 1lb tin loaves or 1 large round loaf)

300g strong wholemeal breadmaking flour

300g strong white flour

Half teaspoon salt

1.5 teaspoons bicarbonate of soda

100g raisins, washed with 1 cup strong tea

1 tablespoon black treacle

400ml buttermilk to glaze

Dangerous
things

The most interesting risk you can take when you have got a bit of a feel for bread making is to abandon the comfort of nice predictable bakers' yeast and venture into the chaos that is wild yeast.

Wild yeasts are all around us all the time. They live on all sorts of grains and fruits and can be coaxed out into a batter of flour and water with a little care and some luck. The most important factor in this arcane art is time. Once you learn to read the signs of fermentation, you will be able to extend the fermentation period to develop the sour lambic and lactic flavours as you prefer.

The dangerous bit is in the delicate balance between a sharp tasty sour, and an overripe dough. An over-fermented sourdough will literally fall apart. The gluten will be destroyed by the acid and your firm, pliant, healthy dough will start to resemble a rough, lumpy porridge.

Think of the sourdough process as a steep hill. The climb is the first bulk rise. It can seem to take forever but this is the key to good sourdough: time equals flavour remember. The downside is that the flavour comes from development of acids which will, if left unchecked, destroy the integrity of the dough. The key is to catch the dough and bake it when the flavours are mature but before the acid destroys the gluten. There is a point where you have to say "This is as late as I dare to leave it", and therein lies much of the fun. As you gain knowledge and experience, you will become a better judge of the time constraints. You will dare to leave the flavours to develop for longer and to extract the maximum taste from the dough. You will know when you do it right. The bread will taste sharp: a fruity sharpness with layers of great fruit, wheat and lactic flavours.

You can avoid the risk of over-fermentation of course. The downside is that your 'sourdough' will taste just as bland and boring as the supermarket pap version. No character, no sourness, no flavour. Why bother? If you are that risk-averse please return to the basic bread section at the beginning of the book until you get bored. Then come back here.

To make it more exciting still, I drop the salt to less than one percent; sometimes less than half a per cent. Partly because I like to push the boundaries and partly because, as you may have gathered by now, I'm not a big salt lover. One of the functions of the salt in the dough is to regulate the enthusiasm of the sourdough culture, so if you reduce the salt you will have less control. The yeast runs wild and creates anarchic hole structures in the crumb. You get huge flavours and really interestingly structural crusts. If you know even vaguely what you are doing sourdoughs will work well most of the time. You will almost never end up with a loaf which is inedible or unpalatable.

It's not really that dangerous at all: a little edgy perhaps, but lots of fun.

You can make a sourdough culture from

anything which can be induced to ferment without the addition of 'bakers' or brewers' yeast. It's not just about wheat.

Traditionally the method is to take wheat grain or wheat flour and add water and warmth to encourage the wild yeasts on the grain to reproduce and start fermentation. Rye grain and flour does this even better than wheat because it ferments happily at room temperature, but we are trying to be a bit more adventurous in this section. It is time to explore in other directions for

interesting starter cultures. Think of all the things that are used around the world to produce wines and other alcohols: grapes obviously, but also apples, pears, barley, even potatoes, rice and cassava. If you can ferment it, you can use it for sourdough culture. We have a damson starter which has a really sharp lambic flavour and runs away to porridge really easily but does make divine rye bread if you have the nerve. Our elderflower starter on the other hand is easy as pie.

Think of the sourdough process as a steep hill. The climb is the first bulk rise. It can seem to take forever but this is the key to good sourdough: time equals flavour

Look in your grandma's recipe book and you will often find a recipe for elderflower champagne, because elderflowers will ferment without any yeast and with little skill required either. Our elderflower culture seems nigh on indestructible. We have done everything to it over the last ten years: frozen it, dried it, added salt by mistake, and yet it still has a beautiful mild creamy flavour and rises strongly and reliably. It makes a cool contrast to the volatility of the damson starter.

If you think it might work just give it a whirl and see what happens. If it doesn't work its cost almost nothing and you have learned a lesson. It is never a waste of time.

The starter recipe and method below uses apples and the indigenous yeasts and *lacto bacilli* which live under the skin. On no account must you peel the apple or it is unlikely to work. This one is usually pretty reliable and I have made lots of starters this way over the years.

First take your apple...
The Apple Sourdough Starter

This starter makes the task of getting a culture to ferment a little easier. The wild yeasts under the skin of an apple are strong and are easily encouraged to express themselves.

The only really important thing to remember is that the apple must not have been sprayed with chemicals, so one from your own tree or that of a friend is a bonus. Failing that, look for an organically-grown one at a local producers' market and question the seller about sprays.

Method

Chop the apple roughly into quarters and crush with the flat of a kitchen knife or a meat tenderizer. Put the apple into the jar. Dissolve the honey or malt extract in warm water and pour over the apple.

Cover the jar with a tea towel or a clean cloth and leave in a warm place for 24 hours. Shake the jar well, cover and leave for 12 hours before shaking again. Repeat twice more.

After this time, the apple should be beginning to break down and should be starting to smell slightly alcoholic, like cider. Inspect the culture for tiny bubbles to confirm that fermentation has begun. If you can't see any bubbles just shake the jar and return to warmth for another 12 hours. Repeat.

If there are bubbles present before you shake the jar, you can start to feed the yeasts with a combination of white flour and warm water.

Mix together 75g white flour and 100ml warm water and add to the jar. Stir the mixture to combine well, then cover with a

Ingredients

1 large unsprayed apple (eaters and cookers are equally suitable)

1 teaspoon honey or malt extract

100ml warm water

A large glass jar with a lid

cloth and return to the warm. Repeat after 12 hours and again after 24.

By this time your culture should be frothy and active.

The next two feeds should be 100g white flour and 100ml warm water, with a 12 hour rest in between. You should now have about a kilo of frothy active culture and it seems ludicrous to throw half of it away, but you need to halve the quantity so that you can feed it four times more. You could give the culture away if any friends are interested in a joint project.

After another 24 hours, you should have a lively culture which is capable of raising a 6kg mix of dough. As a general rule, use three quarters of your culture for the mix and use equal quantities of white flour and water to restore it to its original size. This way the culture stays fresh but also develops the lactic flavours which make the sourdough sour.

A well-kept sourdough culture should be able to live forever, so it's important that the next generation is also schooled in how to maintain it.

I guess that as this section is called 'Dangerous Things', it is a good place to discuss the 'blade on a stick': the lame (pronounced like lamb), of French bakery tradition.

It is also known as a *grignette*, and is for making marks on the crust of the loaf before it goes in the oven. You can use a very sharp knife instead but only real artisan bakers use one of these. There are all sorts of ways to cut the crust and many instruments specially made to do it. Most of them use something very like a good old-fashioned razor blade attached to a pencil-sized handle. The professional bakery versions are usually made from 'detectable' blue plastic, just in case they get dropped into the dough and lost in the production line somewhere!

At home, or in a small artisanal bakery you are very unlikely to misplace your *grignette* and even less likely to have a metal detector as part of your toolkit. In this case the detectable handle is not high on your wants list but the blade usually is, so I'll tell you how many small bakeries make their own *grignettes* for a few pence rather than order the manufactured ones at seven to ten pounds each.

First though, a warning, and a very serious one at that. Please take note and act accordingly or please just use a pair of round-ended safety scissors to make pretty marks on your loaves.

RAZOR BLADES ARE INCREDIBLY SHARP!!!!!!!!!! ("No shit Sherlock!" I hear you cry.) I don't just mean that they are sharp like a sharp knife. Double-edged razor blades are one of those implements that are so sharp that you could (and I have) cut yourself without feeling it at all, until you notice the blood flowing from your hand. Treat razor blades as you would treat broken glass. If you respect how sharp they are and handle them accordingly you will be fine. It's when I'm tired or rushing to make up time lost that I forget I have a blade in my hand and inevitably I end up with another tiny scar to show the next group of students when I'm telling them to be careful with razor blades! It goes without saying, or maybe it doesn't, that you should never leave a *grignette* lying on the worktop. Have a special place for it; ideally high on the wall where no-one can put a hand on it accidentally.

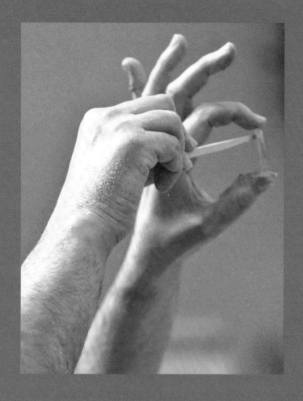

Assuming that you have read and understood the warning I can move on. There are few adequate substitutes for a well-wielded lame when creating the stunning carved crusts you see on many continental, and a few British artisan breads. Lots of other tools will make marks and cuts on the crust: a sharp paring knife, a scalpel, scissors, a serrated tomato knife, etc., etc. None of them offer the same amount of control and flexibility as the razor blade on a stick, so I will tell you how to make one for yourself on the understanding that you will not pass it on without the same warning as you have just read above. This is not a suitable tool for a

minor unless you consider your child would be safe using a cutthroat razor. Your decision to make, but I'd recommend they start with scissors and then progress to a serrated paring knife before you let them anywhere near a *grignette*.

To make your own *grignette* you will need a packet of double-edged 'safety' razor blades and a pencil-sized piece of wood exactly the dimensions of a coffee stirrer from one of the big chains.

To turn this into a *grignette* all you need to do is to bend the blade into a shallow curve between thumb and forefinger and thread the coffee stirrer through the larger slots at each

end of the blade so that it looks a little like a sail on a mast. See the pictures that follow for a better idea of what I mean. It is really important that you flex the blade slowly with your thumb one end and your forefinger the other. Only ever handle the blades with your finger and thumb at either end and you are very unlikely to get cut. Once the blade is on the 'handle' it is safer by virtue of being further from your fingers.

To make the cuts themselves requires practice. The more you use the lame the better you will become, and the more complex your designs can be. Planning is important too. Think of the crust as a canvas and your cut as a brushstroke. The deeper you cut, the broader your line will be when it comes out of the oven. Have an image in your mind of the design you want to achieve so that when you turn the ball of dough out of the rising basket or cloth, 'couchette', you will be able to cut quickly and boldly without wasting too much time getting the loaf in the oven. Begin with just three or four strokes: a triangle, a square or a simple letter perhaps, and work your way to the complex patterns and geometric shapes. The Star of David looks stunning on the top of a beautiful round boule and seems appropriate for a crust decoration to many people too, but you will need lots of practice

before you get it to work perfectly.

I have come to the conclusion that it is not the number of strokes that increases the risk of the pattern vanishing or not working properly. The key factor seems to be the number of intersections of lines and the direction of the cuts to make the intersection. To illustrate this, imagine you have a round boule of dough on the bench in front of you and have decided to mark it with a cross in the centre. You make the first cut: a long straight line over the crown. So far, so good. To maintain the precision of the first cut when you make the second is much more difficult, as the dough will have a tendency to drag when the blade passes through the first line. It will look much better if you cut up to the first line and then turn the loaf through 180 degrees and repeat to make the cross complete. Intersections are always neater and better defined if the cut is made towards the first line and then finished from the opposite side by again cutting towards the first line. To be fair, it's not as important when cutting a simple cross, but when you decide to try your hand at crust calligraphy it will make your letters far more legible and clear cut. Sharp pointed scissors are also useful to help define intricate shapes.

If you are going to be a real artisan bread baker there are a couple of other useful skills to acquire at this stage. The first is proving your loaf in a basket or a *'couchette'* and the second is 'stone baking'.

When your dough has had its bulk proof and you have divided it into suitably sized portions, followed by a thorough kneading and hand-moulding into your desired shape, there are several options available for the final rising stage. The first two are fairly obvious and straightforward: loaf pan or bread tin and baking sheet or baking tray. Both are fine and serve different purposes in the finished loaf of bread, but if you crave more excitement and novelty there are other more traditional techniques.

Baskets, *brotforms*, *bannetons*, or whatever you choose to call them are basically the same thing: a basket made from cane, willow, paper pulp or even plastic, in which to raise the dough.

The Eastern European style, *'brotform'*, tends to be made of willow or cane coiled into a bowl-like basket which leaves a corrugated finish on the crust after proving. These are widely available from suppliers in the UK or the various selling websites like Amazon and eBay. Before use they should be lightly oiled and dusted liberally with flour so that the dough does not stick to the inside after proving. The French style *'banneton'*, is usually a wicker or willow basket lined with heavyweight linen cloth. These too are widely available from the same sources and just need a good dusting of flour prior to each use.

If you are going to use baskets for proving your loaves it is a good idea to buy a good quality stiff bristle hand brush to help keep them clean after you have turned the dough out. Store them in a dry place at room temperature to stop them getting mouldy.

The other option again uses linen but is more versatile in terms of the shapes you are able to achieve. This *'couchette'* is simply a length of finely woven linen cloth. When

dusted liberally with flour, the cloth can be drawn up around the dough to support it while it proves. This is especially useful when you try making baguettes in the traditional way. If you want to try strange-shaped loaves it is wise to use the linen in conjunction with a few bulldog clips or paperclips to hold the linen in the right place.

Basket or cloth proving of the dough is usually the precursor to baking on the hearth or stone floor of a traditional oven. You may aspire to one of these but it is unlikely that you will already have one. Don't despair though, there are other more modest alternatives available to you.

The obvious one is a square or round ceramic tile, usually described as a pizza stone, which is pre-heated in the oven at home before the dough is transferred to it for baking. These seem to work very well and are a great way to start stone hearth baking. The next step is to buy a metal tray the right size for the oven shelf supports and then line it with unglazed ceramic tiles to form a

permanent stone hearth for bread and pizza. The advantage of this is the size of the stone available to bake on, as it extends to the back and sides of the oven. This allows you to bake four loaves at the same time rather than the one you would have room for on the pizza stone.

Another method which works well in my experience is perhaps a little unexpected but worth being prepared for as it is portable so you can take it with you if you make bread away from home too. All you need is a heavy baking sheet (the grill pan which comes with many modern ovens is ideal) and a siliconised baking mat like the ones used by *pâtisseries* to bake delicate pastries without allowing them to stick to the trays. They are available from good quality kitchen suppliers or searchable online. The mat can easily be cut to size for your tray with a pair of kitchen scissors. Line the tray with the silicon mat and pre-heat in the oven from cold just as you would with a pizza stone. The mat allows you to use any metal tray as a stone hearth without the burning of your bread which would result if you put the loaf straight onto hot metal alone. It has worked really well for me at various events where I have had to demonstrate the technique of hearth baking without actually having a stone hearth to bake on. Remember, you heard it here first!

The only thing you now need to know is how to get your beautifully risen and intricately incised artisan loaf to the hearth so you can stone bake it. The professional tool for this task is called a peel, and consists of a sheet usually made of aluminum, but sometimes wood or stainless steel, attached to a short wooden handle. You will be more familiar with peels perhaps in the pizzeria as they are perfect for shoveling pizza into the oven too. Peels are available cheaply online in wood or aluminum, and both can be easily trimmed to suit your oven and your usual loaf size. At the time of writing there are lots for sale online for around £20 each.

If you don't want to buy a peel but still want to have a go and see if hearth baking is for you there is a cheap and easy alternative. You can use a cookie sheet as a peel. A cookie sheet is the type of baking tray which is flat on three edges and has a rim on the other which will allow you to keep hold of the tray as you slide the loaf into the oven to bake. Many people already have one of these baking sheets, but if not they are widely available and inexpensive.

The technique for transferring the risen

dough from basket to oven hearth is simple. When the individual loaf-sized piece of dough is scaled (weighed out) and hand-moulded (shaped), you need to put it gently upside down in the floured basket or *brotform*, so that when it is turned out the tidy side will be on top ready to be cut with your *grignette*.

Sprinkle your peel or cookie sheet with a little polenta or semolina to stop the dough from sticking to it. Turn the dough out of the basket onto the centre of the peel and cut your design into the crust, then transfer the loaf to your 'stone hearth', and bake it as normal. This style of baking is, in my opinion, the opportunity to experiment with your talents and techniques. The crust and its incised decoration are intrinsic to the artisan bread tradition and will impress your family and friends no end as your skills develop.

If you discount the inevitable casual burns you are going to get as you bake, that's about as dangerous as it's going to get.

The Walnut

This does contain walnuts but the name stems from the cut pattern on the crust. I slash it carefully with a razor before it goes into the oven to resemble the pattern on a walnut shell. This loaf is light and full of flavour. It always seems a shame to make it into cheese sandwiches for family lunch boxes but they are the best cheese butties on the planet.

One of my family and customer favourites for nearly 20 years now.

Method

Combine all the dry ingredients in a large bowl and make a well in the centre.

Beat together the eggs, milk, butter and walnut oil and add to the flour with 100ml of water.

Mix by hand until you have a slightly sticky dough, using more water as required. Cover the bowl with plastic wrap or a tea towel and prove in a warm place for two hours.The dough should rise significantly, but rarely doubles in volume.

Turn the dough out onto a well-floured board and knead gently until the dough is soft and elastic. Divide it in two, and shape each half according to your baking tin or basket. If using a basket, line it with a tea towel and dust well with flour. Put the dough into the lined basket with the tidy side facing

Ingredients

350g strong wholemeal flour

150g strong white flour

7g salt

2 teaspoons Fermipan dried yeast

Pinch nutmeg, grated

150g walnuts, shelled

50ml walnut oil

50g unsalted butter, melted

2 large eggs

75ml whole milk

300ml warm water

(you should not need to use all of it)

Additional white flour for kneading and lining the basket

You will also need a willow basket about 20cm in diameter and 10cm deep to rise the shaped loaf in, and a pizza stone for baking it.

The recipe makes two loaves this size so if you have only one basket you can use a well-greased tin for the other half.

down, so that it becomes coated in flour and creates a blank canvas for your cut design.

Heat the oven with the pizza stone inside to 190°C.

Turn out the basket GENTLY onto a polenta-dusted bakers' peel or cookie sheet and score the loaf with a sharp blade to decorate. At first you may be well advised to keep the design fairly simple. As you become more proficient with the blade your imagination may be more expansive.

Slide the loaf from the peel or cookie sheet onto the hot baking stone and bake for 40-50 minutes.

It will sound hollow when knocked on the base if it is done. Cool on a wire rack.

Detox Sourdough

Not an actual detox, but certainly a less rich and complicated alternative to the various cake-like offerings of the Christmas season. Delicious with all those festive leftovers and, if you're still in the mood to party after New Year, perfect for making the bases of canapés which are bang on trend, apparently.

The recipe makes plenty – you'll have enough for a couple of tin loaves and some good rolls so with luck there will be one for the freezer to prepare you for those little emergencies when friends and family descend upon your home without warning.

Method

Mix the dry ingredients in a bowl and make a well in the centre. Add the active sourdough and the yoghurt and mix, adding water as required to make a slightly sticky dough. Make sure that you get all the flour wet. Rye in particular seems to have a knack for remaining dry despite your efforts so I find it helpful to turn the dough completely over at least two or three times during the initial mixing.

Cover the bowl with plastic wrap and leave it to prove somewhere warm for three to four hours.

Turn the dough out onto a floured surface and knead until you have a firm but pliable ball of dough. Prove for an hour.

Oil your tins or baking sheets and divide the dough into pieces to suit your tins.

Knead each piece and shape according to the chosen tin or tray. Brush the top crust with oil if you like it to stay soft, egg white if you don't. Sprinkle with a little coarse sea salt. Prove the loaves in tins or trays for two hours in a warm place.

Heat the oven to 180°C. Bake rolls for 15-20 minutes top of the oven, small tins for 30-35 minutes in the centre and large cobs or bloomers 45-55 minutes on a low shelf. Test by knocking and cool on a wire rack.

If you don't have a sourdough starter you can use regular fresh or dried yeast instead.

This recipe will need 30g fresh yeast or two level teaspoons of Fermipan.

It will improve the flavour and the texture if you make the dough and then keep it in the fridge for a couple of days before dividing and shaping into loaves.

Ingredients

1kg mixed strong white and wholemeal flours

250g rye flour

15g salt

250g active sourdough starter

250g live natural yoghurt

500ml warm water

The Big Boule - Bread for Scouse

If you're baking for a multitude of hungry people, try this recipe for a rye bread to accompany the traditional Liverpool favourite lobskause, or just plain scouse!

The influences behind it were the Germanic/Baltic roots of the dish itself. Following some research it seems that scouse originated with the sailors from Northern Europe who visited Liverpool in the 18th and 19th Centuries.

The most interesting recipe I came across was from the early 19th century and combined large cuts of beef and mutton, cooked together in a vegetable stock. The affluence of the table dictated the proportion of meat to vegetables, but the principle was the same: big cheap cuts cooked for a long time to create flavour and textures in the stew.

I took these pieces of information as my starting point for a suitable bread to grace the scouse table.

To reflect the limitations on the ingredients imposed by budget, I used part wheat and part rye. Rye was a cheaper, coarser grain and was often used with wheat to eke out the household budget. Rye/wheat mixes are very common in Northern Europe and match particularly well with meaty stews and soups.

To reflect the seafaring nature of the origins of lobskause, I used the combination of rye and caraway seed to extend the useful life of the loaf. Caraway adds flavour even to stale bread and the rye makes it retain more moisture and prove more filling and satisfying as a chunk accompanying a big meaty stew like scouse. Just the thing to warm up a crew of hungry sailors in the Atlantic swell.

I have also reflected the time taken in producing a dish of such depth of flavour and texture. The scouse could take all day to prepare so I have allocated a full 14 hours to mix, prove and bake these loaves to let the dough develop more flavour and texture. The steam in the oven will encourage a little spring and a crisp crust to make this bread just perfect for dunking in a big richly-flavoured bowl of lobskause. Here I have used fresh yeast but you could easily substitute a more authentic ale barm or a rye sourdough to make it rise.

The effect of such a substitution would be not only chronological authenticity but would add the sour lambic and lactic flavours to the dough. A worthwhile addition if you have a mind to it!

Method

Mix the dry ingredients together thoroughly in a (very) large bowl and make a well in the middle. Add the liquids and mix until all the flours are wet. Add up to an extra litre of water as necessary to achieve a soft smooth dough. If you are using potato flakes instead of cold mashed potato, you will need more water.

Cover the bowl.

Bulk rise the dough for 12 hours at room temperature.

Remove to a floured board and knead into cobs or bloomers of about 1kg each. Rise on a greased baking sheet at room temperature for 90 minutes.

(You may need to do this in batches more suited to the oven you have available, otherwise some loaves will be very over-risen before baking. It is much better to keep the spare dough in the bulk proving bowl and knead it after a delay of 90 minutes.)

Dust with flour and slash once lengthwise at 45 degrees with a sharp blade. Do not glaze this loaf as it will absorb the scouse juices better without.

Bake for ten minutes at 200°C then release any oven steam and bake at 170°C for 25-40 minutes. This seems like a big variation in baking time but big loaves can be unpredictable. So trust your instincts and knock on the base every five to ten minutes until you are sure.

Cool on a wire rack. Loaves this size,

especially with a high rye content, are exceptional keepers and will make great toast for up to a fortnight.

Obviously you are not confined to scouse to accompany this bread. It is equally at home with other traditional stews and braises. Think of dishes like cassoulet, boiled beef and carrots and Lancashire hotpot.

Ingredients

This quantity will yield about 18 x 1kg loaves. You may want to scale it down a little for domestic use

Per 10kg flour (7kg very strong white bread flour (Carr's Maple Leaf) to 3kg stoneground rye flour (Watermill), you will need;

120g fresh yeast

150g caraway seed

50g cumin seed

50g ground coffee

1.5kg cooled mashed potato (or 1kg potato flake)

125g table salt

4 litres sour milk or buttermilk

500ml vegetable oil

100ml lemon juice

2 litres warm water

Bickering Rolls

Customers, friends and family constantly ask me for chocolate bread so here's a delicious recipe everyone will like. Chocolate and this amount of enrichment will make these fairly slow to rise, so please allow lots of time to make them and try and manage expectations within the tasting queue forming outside the kitchen. The quality of chocolate in this recipe is the key to its success, so get some really top-notch stuff with a high cocoa content. I especially like Montezuma's and Valrhona for these rolls but in any event look for a cocoa solids content of 70-80 per cent, depending on how bitter you like your chocolate.

For an eye-opening taste combination, try a bickering roll with some creamy Gorgonzola or dolcelatte cheese. I know they sound like strange companions but they are surprisingly harmonious together.

These rolls were inspired by the Torinese speciality drink Bicerin which combines coffee, chocolate, cream and hazelnuts. They are meant to be small and delicate, so make lots and keep the family bickering over who gets the last one to a minimum!

Method

Combine all the dry ingredients in a large bowl and make a well in the centre.

Beat the coffee, cream and eggs together in a jug and mix gradually into the flour, adding water as necessary to achieve a soft silky dough. The dough should look dark and shiny.

Cover and set to prove in a warm place for three hours.

Grease or line two baking sheets with parchment.

Beat the remaining egg with one teaspoonful of cold water and reserve for glazing the tops of the rolls. Put the icing sugar into a dredger or a fine sieve for later.

Turn the dough out onto a very lightly-floured surface and knead gently until it feels very smooth and elastic. Divide it into 20 equal pieces of around 50g each and knead each one into an oval roll.

Flatten them one at a time with a rolling pin to a thickness of 2-3mm and roll up quite loosely into a fat cigar shape. Place ten on each tray with as much space all round as possible.

Prove in a warm place for 90 minutes. Heat the oven to 200°C.

The rolls should be well-risen and plump. Carefully brush each one with the egg wash and bake them in the centre of the oven for five minutes, then turn the oven down to 180°C for a further 20 minutes before checking if your rolls are done. The chocolate will still be molten and will burn you so be careful when checking. They smell divine but are best left to cool until just warm before trying one.

It is usually best to hide a couple for yourself at this stage, before they are devoured by your friends and family. Dust with icing sugar and cool on a wire rack.

I'm dubious as to the wisdom of pointing out that rolls as rich as these do freeze remarkably well for up to three months in plastic bags. Try and remove as much air as possible from the bag before freezing. Why am I even bothering to write this down? We all know that you will never ever freeze any of these. They are just too good!

These rolls are delicious warm for breakfast with a coffee or hot chocolate but if you decide to taste them while they are still warm from the oven they may not make it to breakfast.

Ingredients

500g strong white flour

8g salt

1 teaspoon active dried yeast (Fermipan)

50g golden caster sugar

50g cocoa

50g toasted hazelnuts, nibbed (if you choose not to use the nuts, add another 30g chocolate)

50g good quality dark chocolate (70 per cent cocoa solids or more), finely chopped

20g cocoa nibs

150ml espresso coffee, cooled

200ml single cream

2 large free range eggs

250ml warm water (you probably won't need this much)

To finish

1 egg

1 teaspoon cold water

Icing sugar

Stollen

I change my mind about whether I like stollen so often that it makes my head spin. The biggest problem I have with it is the decision to keep what is basically a rich fruit bread for far too long. I prefer my bread fresh, or at least only a week or so old. Stollen tends to be offered for sale after a month or two in the belief that the butter and sugar coating will stop it tasting stale.

I give you the recipe in its entirety, but with a strong recommendation to make your stollen fresh when you want to eat it and to give it only one coat of butter and sugar.

Method

Mix all the dry ingredients in a bowl and make a well in the centre. Add the milk, butter and eggs and combine, then add the soaked fruit and mix into a soft dough. Make sure that all the flour is mixed in thoroughly. Cover with clingfilm and prove for four hours.

Line a large baking sheet with parchment.

Knead the dough on a little flour until elastic and then shape into a long oval loaf. Put it on the baking sheet and brush it with a little melted butter.

Prove in a warm place for an hour and a half.

Heat the oven to 200°C.

Put the loaf in the centre of the oven and turn the temperature down to 180°C.

Bake for 45-50 minutes until golden brown. It should resonate when tapped on the base.

Place the loaf on a wire rack to cool.

Whilst still warm brush with melted butter and dust heavily with icing sugar all over.

(Repeat after 30 minutes and one hour. Repeat after two hours and four hours.)

Wrap the stollen in greaseproof paper and store in a cool environment (not the fridge).

You can stuff the centre of the loaf with 150g marzipan or 75g cinnamon-dusted dried apple for variety.

The apple variant is especially nice with a glass of sherry and a bowl of almonds.

You can keep your stollen for a couple of weeks if you complete the butter and sugar coating.

It does also make an impressive Christmas gift for friends.

Ingredients

The night before baking

50g each of raisins, currants, cherries and
candied peel

4 tablespoons brandy or kirsch

Put in a screw-top jar and shake regularly to
plump the fruit

For the dough

500g strong white bread flour

1 teaspoon dried yeast

50g golden caster sugar

50g toasted flaked almonds

Zest of 1 lemon

10g salt

100g softened unsalted butter

125ml warm whole milk

A few drops of almond essence

2 large eggs

Up to 50ml warm water

To finish

100g melted butter

100g icing sugar

Out there

Things which inspire me to create outstanding Artisan Breads

I own a lot of books. Julie would say I have far too many, especially bread books and recipe books. In fact I don't read the bread books very often. Most of them are just rearrangements of recipes which have gone before and are common knowledge to most bakers. There are a few exceptions, most notably Elizabeth David's 'English Bread and Yeast Cookery' and Richard Bertinet's book 'Dough: Simple Contemporary Bread'. Elizabeth David took over 20 years to write her magnum opus and the detail and history are compelling and interesting when developing new ideas. Richard Bertinet's loaves are some of the best I've ever tasted and his techniques are fascinating in this inspiring book. I also refer to Andrew Whitley's book 'Bread Matters' a lot and would trust Andrew's research above all the scientists ever born! It was eating his Village Bakery bread in the 1970s that got me really interested in experimenting with bread and sourdough and ultimately led to the Staff of Life Bakery.

While I don't read lots of bread books, I do love reading recipe books. I've got hundreds of them. The chefs I find interesting are the ones who are pushing boundaries. They are combining ingredients in new and challenging ways, and using new techniques to alter the tastes and sensations from the raw ingredients. For example, a chef might dehydrate and pulverise pineapple instead of cooking it, as an accompaniment to a pork dish. Dried fruits work well in bread, so it could mean that I can try a pineapple bread specifically suited to bacon sandwiches! It might just inspire me to have a go and see if it works. (It does.)

The cutting-edge chefs today are saying to themselves "Why can't I.....?" in their recipe development. The cocktail bar 'mixologists' are doing the same with their new drinks, playing with dry ice and smoke to change and enhance flavour and the experience of the consumer. At one time there weren't any smoky drinks other than Ardbeg and the other peaty malt whiskies; now you can buy a

> The thing that inspires you mostly is the reaction you get from people when they eat your bread.

'smoking gun' to give your cocktails a whiff of woodsmoke for about £50.

If you want some smoke in your bread you'll have to fill the oven with smoke from a tray of dampened wood chips in the bottom of the oven. Two warnings though. It will fill your kitchen with smoke, so open all the windows before you start. Also, you will need to have a very mild bread dough to be able to taste the smoke, so no strong flavoured ingredients or you'll lose it. The other trendy option is to use smoked flour. It's silly expensive to buy in specialist foodie shops but very easy to smoke your own in a basic homemade cold smoker. For tips Google 'Foodsmoking Jo' Hampson and get the book. Brilliant and inspiring stuff.

Bread is like a big soft blanket that can very easily stifle even quite strong flavours. This is especially noticeable when bakers put chilli in the dough, even in quite big chunks. The flavours are so subdued that you barely notice them until you bite into the centre of a chilli and find a little spice. If you insist on chilli bread, add some complementary flavours like cumin, paprika and cracked black pepper to enhance the dubious experience. Better still, make a huge pan of vegetable or beef chilli stew and dip plain bread into it. The flavours are cleaner and more defined.

I have a big pile of Victorian and Edwardian cookery and baking books which can be good sources of inspiration too. The bakery manuals are very interesting in the range of shapes and recipes from different regions of the UK. Some are shapes that have become really popular in the last century and then disappeared as automation and profit became the driving force in the industry. The cottage loaf is a good example. It is a very attractive shape, but takes care and skill to set properly

to ensure that the smaller bun sits on top of the cob, rather than falling drunkenly to one side. It is also hard to get a cottage loaf to brown evenly, and the texture inside can be ruined by clumsiness in joining the two parts together. You can see how it would not appeal to the mass-market bread factories already. But it's a great British loaf and a piece of our breadmaking tradition so have a go at one and see how you get on.

I found a lovely loaf shape called a 'collar' in one of my Victorian manuals. It is a long oval bloomer with a slash down the centre and a twist of dough running along it from end to end. The collar is a handsome thing indeed, but it occurred to me that it could be the result of an English rural bakery trying to make a 'challah', the beautiful white plait which is so distinctive in the Jewish bakeries of Europe. Nowadays many people would recognise challah just by the name, but my theory is that this baker may have heard about it second- or third-hand from a non-baker and tried to recreate it in his own bakery. The collar is no challah but it is a pleasing shape and a British one. I may well be completely wrong in my conjecture, but it amused me enough to make the loaf more than once and the loaf was good each time.

You can learn loads from reading about how the old bakers and chefs worked their magic. They weren't using all the sophisticated equipment we use nowadays, nor did they have an array of chemicals to do the work for them. Their techniques are much more akin to today's real artisans than those of the big 'craft' bakeries. The big producers use so much industrial plant machinery and so many chemical compounds and undetectable enzymes in their production processes that they are no use as inspiration, even if they were making bread you would want to eat! Whether you want to do what they do or not is immaterial – you just can't. But the old guys mixed big doughs by hand, moulded by hand and then baked in big wood- or coke-fired ovens, whose temperatures are within the range of many domestic ovens. It is perfectly feasible to do it how the Victorian baker did it. You already have most of the equipment you're going to need.

Some of the best quality free-thinking inspiration comes from baking with children, because they have no inhibitions about what you can include in a bread recipe! I run lessons in local schools now and then where the children have to design and bake a loaf for themselves. The age group is usually nine or ten years old. In the same situation a student or an adult would go first to other people's recipes for

some guidelines. Children don't do that: they go first to their own imagination, and then they stay there until the job's done. It's a recipe for chaos, but from chaos comes the really innovative thinking. I tell the class what needs to be in the bread to make it work: flour, water yeast and salt. Then I give them complete licence to do whatever they like. Two little boys once baked a loaf with a handful of fizzy sweets inside. It was one of the most hideous-looking things I've ever

seen, as it popped and oozed lurid slime from a hundred orifices. Two girls dyed their loaf blue with food colouring to make it more interesting for the class. It was interesting, but no-one wanted to eat it as it just looked too weird.

The best experiment came when two pupils took an orange and just chopped it roughly into about sixteen pieces and mixed it into the dough, pith and peel included. The bread was delicious and had risen beautifully, with the orange flavour and scent permeating the whole loaf. I was thrilled with it and we have made it at the bakery many times since, using spiced kumquats instead of the oranges. Now and then we all need to get into the mindset where we can think like a child. Instead of saying "why should I put that in?" we need to ask "why can't I?"

I'm firmly convinced that the thing which should inspire you most in your breadmaking is the reaction you get from others when they eat your loaves. The whole idea of making bread is to eat it yourself and to share it with others. That is why we all do it; it's not just for showing off, is it?

Although I did once bake an eight-foot long snake loaf for a show, which had a hosepipe inside to hold it together! Needless to say, I neither ate it myself nor did I share it. Probably just as well.

Perfect partners

A few of my favourite ways to use bread to present food, to complement food, to accompany food, and above all, to show off.

Just because the received "wisdom" says that if you are eating *pâté de foie gras* you must have brioche doesn't make it so. I like foie gras and I like brioche but together I find them a little dull. Foie gras is so rich and smooth that to pair it with a rich smooth bread like brioche seems to be missing an opportunity to introduce some contrast. I like it much better with a dark grainy wholemeal bread with a thick chewy crust. It emphasises the smoothness of the rich foie gras with its coarse textures and the stronger wheat flavours of wholemeal. As I have said earlier, I love to try something different. If you like *pâté de foie gras* try it with wholemeal for a change. If you prefer it with brioche at least you have thought about the combination rather than just accepting it blindly.

Refuse to be confined by the conventions as some of them are just plain daft. Experiment with your palate and your preferences before you decide.

There is a trend for eating Irish soda bread with smoked salmon. I find soda bread tastes too chemical for me, so unless the salmon is a very strong peat smoked variety I'd rather have real bread or ideally some rye sourdough or black bread. I can see that the tradition of eating smoked salmon with soda bread has come from pairing the preferred breads of the UK's smoked salmon producing areas (Ireland and Scotland), with the indigenous salmon. It's logical to a point but the logic has a flaw. Soda bread as a style was unknown before the widespread use of household baking soda became feasible in the 1860s. The preservation of salmon by smoking is a much older process whose origins are incredibly ancient. It is worth asking whether the symbiosis of smoked salmon and soda bread was more indicative of the fondness of the Irish fishwives for their wheaten and treacle breads, than of any real affinity between the two flavours.

If you are making bread in a distinct style, it helps to think of the complementary cuisine of that country. If you are baking sour Scandinavian rye bread, for instance, you think of gravadlax, wild mushrooms, game and fish. French *pain ordinaire* is delicious with strong soft cheeses and tasty pâtés, Italian *pane Toscano* with olives, salt and ripe tomatoes. It's obvious, once you apply your commonsense.

Some flavours are made for each other.

Oranges and walnuts, for instance, with good dark chocolate is a match made in Heaven. My other favourite is caraway and bacon, especially when lightly smoked. Alsatian and German cuisine has been putting these flavours with cabbage for centuries. It's not new, just a prompt so that you can hone your instincts for matching flavours to create a harmonious whole. At the risk of sounding like Yoda, you must learn to trust your own senses rather than bow to convention.

Here are a few combinations which we really like.

Peanut butter, banana and jam on brioche.

Is it a posh sandwich? Of course it is! Bread is brilliant at adapting to its environment and can make your sandwiches as posh as you like. It will be a bacon sarnie of doorstep proportions on a Saturday night, or masquerade as a witty canapé which will make adults smile and remember their childhood.

These sandwiches are made with the Light Brioche loaf on page 46 and are cut to be only 2cm square, but there's nothing stopping you from playing with the size and

shape until it makes you happy. The rich brioche works really well with the filling. It's almost like a sandwich cake. Try these when the kids are out or they'll steal them all.

Try and get one of the less salty and sugary crunchy nut butters or make your own with a stick blender. If you fancy a change use pistachios instead of peanuts: much better, but pricy!

Slice the banana if you want pretty, but really any kid will tell you they are better mashed. Then choose your jam. Homemade or a good bought one. We like blackcurrant best but with pistachios I'd have cherry instead. Like Cleopatra the allure of these lies in their infinite variety.

Brioche chips with melted chocolate and vanilla salt.

We had a play on the theme of 'chips and dips' which went to my favourite of French fries and aioli and then to this. A tin loaf of brioche is cut into 'chips' as chunky as you like. Ours were at the French fries end of the scale because the dishes for dipping were small and the chocolate was Montezuma's 73% cocoa solids couverture. It comes in giant buttons and melts beautifully with a rich warmth of flavour without the bitterness of some dark chocolates. We simply melted the couverture and poured it into a cup, then sprinkled it with some vanilla-infused sea salt crystals to make a contrast in the texture and

flavour. They look fantastic, are dead easy to make and will keep your guests entertained over coffee. If you served potato French fries with a Mexican mole dip to begin with it would raise a few eyebrows! Why not?

Herb pots with celeriac and smoked mackerel.
The recipe for these Italian-inspired herb and olive oil bread bowls is on page 53.

We bake it in a small straight sided tin. You could use a small baked bean tin if you cut off the top and bottom and line it with parchment paper then put it on a baking sheet to go in the oven. As long as it ends up as a cylinder that you can hollow out, it will be fine.

Cut the top off and reserve, then cut out the crumb and put it aside to make into crumbs for home made fishfingers (Panko? Not for me thanks.) You now have a little pot with a lid. Make your celeriac into a rémoulade with some decent mayonnaise or aioli and fill the pot, then put a piece of the mackerel over the top. Put the lid on top of the fish too if you like. It is delicious and you get to eat the dish too! If you want to take them on a picnic, use a little less rémoulade and get the fish inside the bowl too. Put the lid on and tie it with string or ribbon so it won't fall open and spill.

If you intend to use bread bowls with a moist hot filling like scrambled eggs and smoked salmon or goulash, you will need to brush the inside with a little olive oil and return it to a hot oven (180°C) for ten minutes to seal and then allow it to cool before filling. This will make it more resistant to the liquid, but not waterproof, so do not fill the bowls until just before you take them to table. In these cases I think they look best with the lids put back on.

Herb bread with chorizo, caper berry and Manzanilla de Sanlúcar de Barrameda sherry.

The 'lid' that we cut off the bread bowl previously was used to make a very easy but classy tapas dish. Quite appropriate that we should use the lid of our bread bowl for a tapa, as the original meaning of tapas is thought to refer to a cover or lid, over a glass of sherry. The 'lid' was usually made of bread or ham: a great combination with a glass of sherry.

To make these, just fry some diced or sliced chorizo in its own fat until just starting to turn brown, then add a tablespoon of robust red wine, to deglaze the pan and coat the chorizo. Lightly toast the 'lid' on both sides and top the flat side with chorizo and a little of the pan juices. Add a big caper berry and serve as an appetiser with a cool glass of Manzanilla sherry. The flavours combine really well to get you ready for dinner. You could, of course, just use slices of *pain ordinaire* rubbed with a little olive oil before grilling when you run out of lids from the bread bowls.

Wholemeal lemon sandwiches.

Sandwiches again? Yes. Posh ones again? Possibly. Delicious and totally unexpected? Absolutely!

Our classic OMG Wholemeal loaf is definitely my favourite bread ever. It's dark from the molasses and nutty from the pumpkin, sunflower, linseed, poppy, hemp and sesame seeds in the mix. Wonderful with all sorts of other foods, it lifts smoked salmon to a level bordering on sublime, but in this recipe, I'm pairing it with an unexpected partner: lemon.

The type of lemon is important. Choose the big, thorny Amalfi lemons which have a fairly

short season in the UK. Look out for them in March until the end of the summer. They are unwaxed, so they have a short shelf life, but the scent which comes off them says quite clearly "Eat me now!" so just buy them when you need them. Amalfi lemons are super-fragrant, and have a mildly acidic character with a huge lemon flavour that makes them the favourite of chefs all over the world.

These sandwiches are so simple that you will be amazed how good they are.

Slice the wholemeal bread thinly, no more than four millimetres. Spread lightly with good unsalted butter and top with two millimetre slices of lemon, rind and all. Make into elegant sandwiches and then try not to wolf the lot before you get the chance to share them. The lemons taste sweeter if you add a pinch of coarse sea salt to the sandwich. I prefer them sharp, so I leave the salt out. If you're serving smoked salmon in the summer, include a few of these on each plate. Amalfi lemon sandwiches are lush.

Walnut bread with walnuts, pears and Roquefort.
I adore walnut bread like the one on page 82 partly because it is so versatile. The kid in me, however, adores it because it goes ever so slightly purple due to the dyeing effect of walnut skins. It's barely discernible, but when you glimpse it from the edge of your vision, that bread is definitely purple and that makes me happy.

This combination is a classic French lunchtime plate. Ripe fresh pears, earthy walnuts and the sharp tang of Roquefort ewe's milk cheese. What's not to like? The only thing it lacks is a good slice (or four) of crusty,

flavoursome fresh baked real bread. If that bread is almost but not quite purple it adds to the colour, the flavour and the texture of the other ingredients.

The only thing you need to do is slice up the ingredients and arrange them nicely on a board or a platter. Simple.

Whole rye bread with smoked salmon pâté and hot smoked salmon flakes.

Playing with my food again! We were all told off for it when we were children but for entertainment value it takes a lot of beating. The starting point for this was some stunning photographs of traditional handmade Japanese sushi. The simplicity of the forms was interesting and inspiring. Our 'sushi' isn't boiled rice. It's tiny blocks of rye bread, made from our own damson sourdough starter with coarse organic rye flour, and a little treacle to make it dark and sticky.

We cut the rye bread into small blocks, then topped each one with smooth smoked salmon pâté. The bit on the top is hot-smoked, or smoke-roasted salmon. Cold-smoked salmon is cured, rather than cooked. Hot-smoked is smoked and roasted at the same time. The texture is very different: more like regular roasted salmon but with a whiff of oak smoke.

When you get really great nigiri sushi there are different textures in each mouthful: the rice, sticky and a little granular; the fish, meaty and clean-tasting; and then a combination of wasabi paste and *shoyu* which is smooth and full of flavour. That is where the motivation came from for this presentation. It's not sushi, that was just the inspiration. This has its own character, flavours and

textures. I borrowed the bamboo mat from Japanese cuisine too and I'm really happy with the way it turned out. I think you could take these anywhere and people would be amazed by them. There are three very distinct flavours and textures in each one and I think they look super-cool too.

Wholemeal with Cumbrian beef, rocket and wasabi.

Here's my OMG Wholemeal again; the one I made the Amalfi lemon sandwiches with. The meat is an almost raw seared fillet of Cumbrian beef from Chris, my butcher.

Compare that to the greyish slices of what is euphemistically labelled 'cooked beef' in your local supermarket. That label 'cooked beef' hides a multitude of sins, I'm sure. The stuff is bland as anything and has the texture of blotting paper: you don't so much cut it as break it.

Chris's beef, on the other hand, is so well-reared and cared for that I'd happily eat it raw. The texture is how great steak should be, tender and juicy. A flash in a red-hot pan is just enough to seal the outside and add a hint of caramelisation. Cut it as thick as you please; as thick as your finger or as thin as prosciutto, then wrap it in spicy, peppery rocket and dot it with fiery Japanese wasabi paste before making your sandwich. Fabulous as a doorstep buttie when you are

ravenously hungry, but try it at your next party cut down thin to a one-bite sandwich canapé. It's delicious and impressive to those who value flavour, texture and integrity in their food. Those who don't are unlikely to be at your party in the first place. All the components have to be good though. The best bread you can make, meat with a provenance from a butcher who cares whether you come back for more, fresh rocket and wasabi made up fresh from powder to keep its bite. This is strong stuff but satisfying.

Anyone for a panko-encrusted deep fried cherry mozzarella *bocconcini* with white chocolate and smoked oatmeal houmous dip? I thought not!

A quick word about dipping your bread.

Often in would-be Mediterranean restaurants when I ask for bread I am presented with a basket of average white frozen baked-off baguette. Fair enough, I asked for it. I should have guessed. Even worse is the common condiment presented alongside it in a dull small round dish which ten years ago would have been an ashtray. The dish should alert you to this bistro's shortcomings even if the pseudo-baguette did not. The clincher is when you see a blob of dark liquid crouching malignantly below a pool of indifferent cooking oil from the kitchen. "Olive oil and balsamic, sir?" Er… no, thanks! The "balsamic" bears no resemblance to the sweet, unctuous aged vinegar from Modena so presumably it is simply balsamic acid, like a bread-dipping equivalent of non-brewed condiment from the last resort chip shop. The fact that it lurks under the tasteless olive oil is actually a bonus, as you will only manage to get "balsamic" on your bread by soaking up a huge amount of oil in the attempt and hopefully give up on the whole operation.

In restaurants where they are careful in selecting quality olive oil and genuine balsamic vinegar to complement it, you will never see them in the same dish. Oil and vinegar come separately because they don't mix. Its better that way so you can savour the smell and the taste of the oil and then move on to the rich smooth acidity and fruity sweetness of the balsamic vinegar.

The discussion above prompted me to find the condiments I would want to dip my own breads into before a meal and add them to this little list of suggestions for your entertainment.

I started with a tiny bottle of 25-year-old balsamic vinegar from Modena which cost a fortune and was a present from a good friend. It pours like syrup and has layers of flavour all the way from sharp acidity to sweet figs and raisins.

The olive oil in this case was a lemon and black pepper-infused olive oil from Naomi at Agnes Rose. It was fresh and grassy but with a zesty lemon taste and a hint of cracked pepper. Really very sophisticated and fun.

I chose a balsamic vinegar from Agnes Rose too. This was the Lyth Valley damson-infused one, with plummy damson taste to bring out the fruit elements of the balsamic grape flavours.

The trio worked really well to emphasise fruit and fresh flavours without heavy, mouth-coating oiliness from poor olive oil or sour stinging acid from cheap vinegar. Rather than the ubiquitous semi-freddo baguette, I chose the three breads I'd been using for the other elements, and tried to match them to the dips. The herb and olive oil bread worked very well with the fruity aged balsamic and I teamed the walnut bread with the lemon zest in the olive oil infusion. Walnuts and lemons are natural companions so my wholemeal bread was left with the damson-infused balsamic vinegar. A surprising combination but worked really very well, with the dark sugars in the loaf emphasising the damson fruits in the vinegar. I'm not saying this is the definitive combination which suits all breads or all diners, just that the combination of other ingredients deserves a little thought, and merits some consideration in the choice of bread too.

Use this chapter, and indeed this whole book, as a springboard for your own leaps of faith in your own talent. If you take anything away from the reading of it, I'd like that to be a healthy disrespect for baking convention and received wisdom. Find that inner child who says "Why can't I.......?" and indulge them a little until you start to see the limits only when you look back behind you.
Happy baking.

Good
companions

Those friends with whom I love to break bread

A companion is, quite literally, someone to break bread with. It comes from the Latin *'cum panem'* which means 'with bread'. Colloquial French uses the word *copain* to mean a close friend, obviously sharing the same etymological roots.

Sharing bread is one of the most fundamental expressions of humanity, and tearing your own bread in half to feed your friend is truly companionship. Your breadmaking skills may become staggeringly sophisticated and refined but, for me, it's all about the people you choose to share it with. Friends, family, neighbours, chefs, and then customers when I decided to go professional, are a huge part of why we choose to create food.

I know it sounds a bit cheesy, but real bread and cheese have always been a perfect combination!

We are right at the other end of the scale from the 'Family Bakers since 1876' bread factories. We spend time together socially and celebrate family occasions in each other's homes and families all the time. The people who work with me are family as far as I'm concerned. We work hard together rather than them working for me - I'd never think of describing them as staff. I only hear that term applied to bakers by the born managers who don't want to bake themselves. I don't have a single managerial bone in my body - I want to bake bread. Someone once asked me what I'd do if I won the lottery and I came to the

"Sharing bread is one of the most fundamental expressions of humanity"

Ali with baby David

Kev

Jaro

Jana

conclusion that I'd still have to bake. I'd have to give the bread away because I can't stop baking but I wouldn't need the money for it.

Staff of Life has been a family affair right from the beginning. Started by me and my wife Julie, we soon had Julie's brother Kev and her parents, Jean and Mike, working there too. Jean and Mike enjoyed the atmosphere of the bakery until they were both in their eighties, then came in when they were passing just for a chat. Shortly afterwards Stefan joined us every now and then just because he could see we needed a hand and loves making bread. I don't think I've taught Stefan anything. He has an instinctive feel for the dough and, like me, he can tell if it's not right just by handling it for a moment. I honestly don't think we could have managed without him all these years. Stefan is definitely family, and his charming daughters Rosa and Bella have both worked behind the counter at Staff of Life too.

The family extended a little when Jaro joined us and I taught him from scratch how to make real Artisan bread. Jaro is from Slovakia, and had no background in baking or catering at all. This proved to be a blessing as it meant that he wasn't tied to already-learned 'rules' about technique and yeast/salt proportions. He is now a great baker, instinctive and insightful and making the bread just as I do. We had some fun at the beginning trying to communicate by drawing pictures in the flour on the bench, but his English is much better these days. He was soon joined by his partner Ali who is a tiny dynamo in the bakery, making delicious cakes in ever-larger batches as customers try them and become addicted. Ali's daughter Jana and her fiancé Lubos became an important part of Staff of Life too and are now running the bakery full-time, whilst Julie and I take on new challenges. Jana and Lubos have both been trained in cooking and pâtisserie, so they are bringing new ideas and recipes to the repertoire alongside the old favourites.

Me and Julie

Me and my
friend Aidan
judging a
baking
competition

The bakery is a moving balance between our two families and that is as it should be. As we get older it is time for new ideas and fresh viewpoints. My son loves bread but he will never want to be a baker. He has helped us in the bakery and is often on hand to help me when I give demonstrations at events, but his heart lies in the theatre and I have to respect his passion. I recognise the dedication and single-mindedness I see in my own character applied to artisan bread, so I support him 100 per cent in his choice.

Jaro and Ali, Jana and Lubos are almost like our adopted family too. We want them to succeed and build the business so we have to give them the freedom to do it with our support and encouragement. Maybe one day Jana's son David will be a real artisan baker too, like the rest of the family. He certainly enjoyed his first Staff of Life picnic at Windermere.

Joe and me

Trusted sources

Sources you may find helpful

Carrs Milling. Silloth and Kirkcaldy

Carrs produce a varied range of flours especially for bread making including the "Breadmaker" range for home use with bread machines. Carrs flours are the mainstay of Staff of Life and many other good artisan bakeries around the country. We value their consistent protein level and their exceptional customer service. When reproducing recipes is important we turn to Carrs.

Gilchester Organics. Northumberland

Gilchesters are our nearest growers of fine breadmaking wheats and other grains. They also mill their own products so we can rely on their organic status from field to bakery. We especially like Gilchesters spelt wholemeal flour for a lovely nutty flavour with caramel notes which gives a nice sweetness to the finished loaf without adding lots of sugar or honey. We also like their light rye and 100 per cent rye flours for pure rye and multigrain loaves.

The Watermill. Little Salkeld, Cumbria

The Watermill is our nearest mill. Restored in the 1970s by Nick and Ana Jones, it is a fully working water-powered mill, producing a range of biodynamic flours and cracked grains to Demeter standard. We use their spelt wholemeal, coarse rye, medium rye and 100 per cent wholemeal flours plus cracked wheat and rye.

Suma Wholefoods Cooperative. Leeds

Suma is one of those wholesalers who buck the trend for big food suppliers cutting costs and quality in order to maximise profit for shareholders. An ethically inspired cooperative, Suma is a lot of fun to have as a supplier. They source top quality ingredients from ethical sources around the world and deliver nationwide.

Montezuma's Chocolate

We tried most of the chocolate available before choosing Montezuma's for our Three Chocolate Bread. The ones we use regularly for bread and for cakes are the dark chocolate, milk chocolate and white chocolate couverture. For a real chocolate flavour that won't get lost in the bread Montezuma's 73% cocoa solids dark couverture ticks all the boxes. All their chocolate range is ethically sourced and Fairtrade accredited.

Mark Clegg Cheese Wholesale. Preston

We have dealt with Mark Clegg's Cheese for

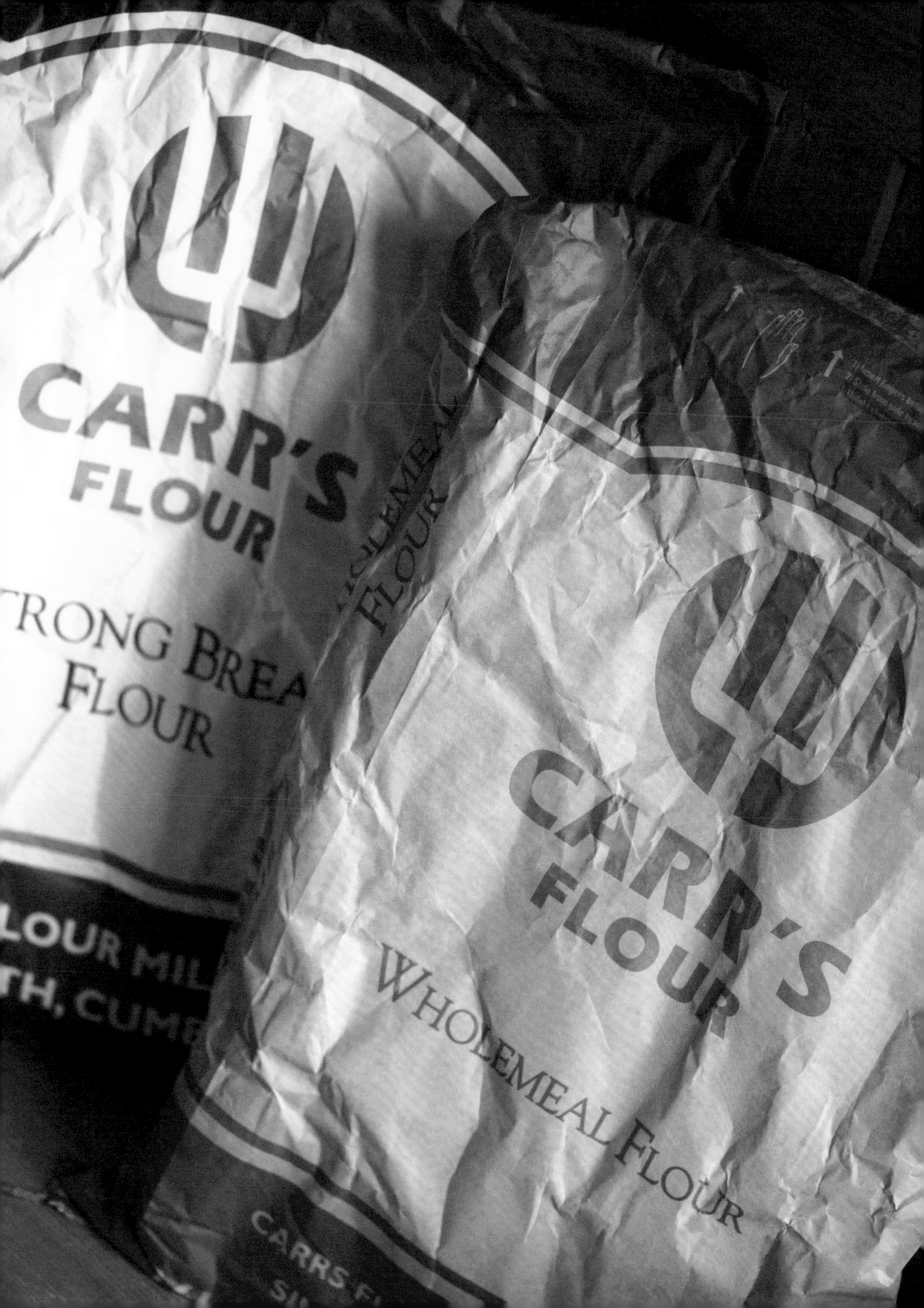
CARR'S
FLOUR
FLOUR
CARR'S
FLOUR
WHOLEMEAL FLOUR

years and depend on their brilliant customer service for most of our cheeses for baking. There seems to be no dairy or charcuterie product they can't find and deliver with no drama or fuss. We use Reggiano Parmesan and extra mature cheddar every day and special orders when I have a rush of blood (or possibly milk) to the head and a new bread is born.

Thornby Moor Dairy. Cumbria

Barbara and Leonie produce our favourite cheeses from their dairy in the north of the Lake District. We especially love their Cumberland Farmhouse and its smoked version. Both are big flavours in a full fat hard cheese which matures beautifully and deserves a place on any cheeseboard. Their soft fresh and rind washed cows and goats milk cheeses are equally delicious.

Cartmel Cheeses. Cartmel, Cumbria

As well as being a great cheese shop in the pretty Lakeland village of Cartmel, Martin Gott's former shop also stocks his own ewes milk rind washed cheese, St James. Absolutely delicious with a nice rich fruit bread.

Agnes Rose. Kendal, Cumbria

Naomi Darbishire produces the best fruit-infused oils and vinegars we have ever tasted from her premises in Kendal. For dipping your wonderful homemade artisan breads you deserve something a little more special than the average balsamic vinegar and olive oil. Try Agnes Rose Cumbrian Damson Balsamic and their lemon-infused olive oil. You will never go back!

Montezuma's®
innovative british chocolate

Booths Supermarkets. North of England

It may seem strange to find an endorsement for a supermarket in this book, but if you know Booths you will understand. Booths has been described as the Waitrose of the north but for us they are more like a very good local grocer. The customer service is outstanding and they go out of their way to source local and unusual products of genuine quality. If we didn't think they were a brilliant company there's no way we would have supplied Booths with Staff of Life Bread.

Cooks at Carlton. nr Snaith, Yorkshire

At the beautiful and historic Carlton Towers in Yorkshire, Lord Gerald Fitzallan has created a cookery school which makes an occasion of a one-day cookery course.

The old kitchens have been transformed into a state of the art learning environment for up to twelve students for a wide range of courses including Artisan Bread, Afternoon Tea, Game Preparation and many more. The bonus is the lovely house itself, the perfect hosting skills of Elaine and the team and the wonderful lunch prepared for you by the indispensable Julie. Truly an unforgettable experience.

Carvettii Coffee. Cockermouth, Cumbria

Gareth and Angharad carefully select small batches of beans from the best estates around the world and roast them slowly and with an obsessive dedication to extract the flavours which reflect the best characteristics of the coffee. This particular "madness" results in coffee with the sophistication of fine wine and lends itself well to experiments in food-matching which guarantees surprises.

And Also...

All the Real Artisans out there producing wonders in whatever field they excel.
I applaud you all and sincerely hope that I will get a chance to meet at least some of you and try your wares. You are brilliant examples of what England does so well. That touch of apparent madness which makes you obsessive about quality and authenticity is the touch of genius which makes you amazing. People like us make it fun to be alive and the more you meet, the more you appreciate your own skill, dedication and value. Over the years I have met many wonderful makers in many different fields. Each occasion is an affirmation of my own decision to do it my way. I have been foraging in the woods of the Lake District with Fergus Drennan and Ben McNutt of Woodsmoke Bushcraft. I hand-forged a carving axe under the tutelage of Dave Budd in Devon. I've smoked every food you can think of following an incredible day spent with 'Foodsmoking Jo' Hampson and her partner Georgina.

All these people are possessed of comprehensive knowledge and legendary skills in their crafts and time spent in their company is education in the best possible sense. I thoroughly recommend that you seek out the best to learn from. Even if you are not an obsessive axe-forger (and trust me, I'm not), the experience of working alongside the world-renowned bladesmith Dave Budd will expand your horizons no matter who you are.

Real Artisans are not that easy to find using only the internet, as many of them either don't want or don't need the extra exposure to make a living. Personal recommendation from someone you trust or respect is still the best strategy to avoid wasting your money. The real experts tend not to be on websites and forums blowing their own trumpets, but if you ask for recommendations the same names will keep on coming up.

Your most trusted source should always be your own taste and your instincts. If the Sunday supplements are celebrating a new hand-ground coffee which has been part-digested by a Scandinavian wombat to justify the horrific price tag, go with your instinct to laugh out loud at the fools so easily parted from their money! In my experience there are many instances when the best is very definitely not the most expensive and few, if any, when it is. I look for passion and commitment over smart marketing and taste always triumphs over cool packaging concepts.

I'm sure you all know one or two people like my Real Artisans. The good thing is that they will be able to point you to others in your area and so your journey goes on. Enjoy the journey and in time you will realise that there is no destination, just a feeling of being incredibly privileged to be part of this wonderful culture and philosophy: the creation of excellence.

First published in Great Britain in 2015 on behalf of:
Staff of Life – www.staffoflifebakery.co.uk
2 Berry's Yard, Kendal, Cumbria, LA9 4AB
Tel: 01539 738 606

Published by: RMC Books – www.rmcbooks.co.uk
6 Broadfield Court, Sheffield, S8 0XF
Tel: 0114 250 6300

Text © Simon Thomas, 2016
Design © RMC Books, 2016
Photography © Jodi Hinds (www.jodihinds.com), 2016

Author: Simon Thomas
Design: Dan Wray
Editors: Adam Kay, Martin Edwards

Printed and bound in Great Britain by CPI Colour Ltd.

A CIP catalogue record for this book is available
from the British Library.

ISBN: 978-1-907998-23-2